Losing It in France

Losing It in France

Les Secrets of the French Diet

Sally Asher

NH
NEW
HOLLAND

To my husband, Simon, and to our children Matilda and Alfie — nothing tastes as good as your love feels.

To my mother, Judy — you have always strived to give me the best you know, but most of all, you believe in me.

Contents

Acknowledgements

To all of the team at New Holland Publishers, particularly my editors Diane Jardine and Mary Trewby. Thank you for your belief, hard work and dedication in bringing this book to life.

To Josianne for being a positive role model and for the valuable skills I learnt from you.

Introduction

There is something magical about France, and especially about Paris, that defies description. Ambience, charm, chicness, history, colour, architecture, fashion—the list goes on. Paris is a complete feast of beauty. People fall in love with this city for their own personal reasons.

For me, it was love at first bite. Nothing gets my heart racing like my love of French food. What I find most enticing is the ability of the French to elevate food and wine to an art form—and pamper themselves by indulging selectively, yet still ensure they look spectacular in a Chanel suit. After all, image is everything, especially in Paris. The French seem to break every rule of modern diets and remain effortlessly slim. In other countries, the more obsessed we are with thinness and dieting, the fatter we become.

Rather than spend hours sweating on a treadmill, the French seem to be able to easily balance food, lifestyle and movement, which allows them to eat what they really want and stay slim without resorting to crazy extremes. While falling in love with France—and a Frenchman—I simultaneously fell in love with my tastebuds, believing like the French do that managing my weight need not be torturous, but rather a love affair with our five senses.

Eating, for the French, is a sensual experience, not a fearful one. Just like a sommelier tastes fine wine, I learned to savour the varied tastes, textures and aromas of the food I ate. By being fully present while eating, in both heart and mind, I began to hear the subtle, inner symphony of pleasure, which taught me so much about feeling truly satisfied. And I realised that in the past I had done a lot of swallowing, but not much tasting. For years I had regularly eaten my sorrows, my fears, my past and my future. I got all the calories but without the bliss. Yet, just by closely studying the habits of all the slim French people, I came to understand that managing your weight can be fun and even indulgent. After all, if you want to find out how to do something, it's best to learn it from those who do it best.

My firsthand observations, while living with a traditional French family in Paris, gave me the invaluable gift of freedom: freedom from ever dieting again. By learning to recognise and respect my internal cues of hunger and satiety, I began to listen to my body. By allowing myself to eat previously forbidden foods, I discovered there was no reason to eat them all at once when I knew I could have them again later. By slowing down my eating pace, I learned to truly savour every morsel and to be fully in-the-moment while eating. Although I ate less, I actually enjoyed food a whole lot more. I was relieved to discover you don't have to give up sumptuous foods to be slim and healthy.

You can learn these French lessons too. Adapt them to your own environment, lose weight and keep it off for life. And not with a scowl on your face but with the blissful smile of a Cheshire cat.

In France, the epitome of *la belle vie* (the good life) is food—the great ice-breaker that brings people together and makes life more pleasurable, moment by moment. The French agree that food is sacred and that eating must be undertaken with great respect and ceremony. I was fascinated by how the French focus pure loving attention on their meals, cooking and eating only the freshest, best ingredients. All over the country, you find patisseries selling mouthwatering gateaux and warm baguettes on one corner and on the next, a café where the French linger over *un café* for hours, taking their time, simply contemplating life. France is known for rich desserts, foie gras, full-fat cheeses, charcuterie and wine, yet most people seem to have little trouble maintaining a healthy weight.

It's been called the French paradox—and I was determined to get to the bottom of it.

I am not French, nor was I born in France. So I didn't have my tastebuds trained from a young age or any secret well-honed tricks passed down from generation to generation instilled in the crib. Instead, I had to change several decades of dreadful dietary habits—habits that were preventing me from reaching and maintaining my ideal weight. But I did change for the better and the results have lasted.

Ironically, the secret to losing weight and keeping it off did not involve applying aggressive discipline and deprivation—it was about believing that I deserved to love what I eat and eat what I love. I learned to distinguish between physical hunger and psychological hunger, respect fullness, and eat with pure awareness. I replaced self-criticism with self-nurturing. I embraced the concept of quality over quantity and learned to go that extra mile to make each meal special. The French believe good food is their birthright and adopting this concept led me on a pleasurable journey to spoiling myself thin.

You don't have to speak French, or even go to France, to do what I did because once you learn the principles of eating and moving like the French—with balance, variety and moderation—you can adapt them to any geographical environment.

The experience of living with a family in Paris gave me an insight into how the French eat at home every day. I realised that it is not just about what you eat (although good nutrition is important). Understanding how and why you eat is a key factor in achieving lasting weight loss. By giving myself permission to eat what I had spent years trying to avoid, I began to derive great pleasure from small quantities and eat without guilt, while staying attuned and responsive to my inner satiety cues. As the French remain a culture motivated by the pleasures of good food, I too acquired a deeper appreciation of quality, freshness and flavour in my food, along with the ceremony and pleasure taken at mealtimes.

In Paris I discovered a rhythm of life and a relaxed attitude that allowed me to say yes to all the foods I love, yet still lose weight without any blood, sweat or tears. Without ever feeling deprived, I managed to lose the elusive ten kilos I had been wrestling with for years. I realised that lasting and permanent weight loss is more involved than simply following a calorie-controlled meal plan, because we need to become adept at nourishing not only our body but also our mind, heart and spirit. I had to learn what to do when I thought I was hungry but when, in truth, what I really needed was not food.

The French stay slim not because they are genetically blessed but, quite simply, because of the difference in their culinary attitudes and dietary habits. They have a mindset that helps them stay slender and they refuse to accept that being overweight has to be part of their fate. When food is viewed as a pleasurable source of sustenance rather than used as a coping mechanism, there is never a valid reason to eat more than the body needs at any given time. It seems that a positive self-image and a healthy level of self-acceptance towards your own body and beauty are very useful if you want to fight the flab. When you embrace your body image and accept your genetic blueprint, you are more easily able to master the art of intuitive self-care. The

French know how to love themselves, flaws and all. It's no secret that they want to be beautiful, in love, feel sexy and take care of themselves so they look good.

Not surprisingly, seduction and flirting are art forms in France. They love to engage in flirtatious behaviour every day, so feeling good in your own skin is of the utmost importance. I remember the look of alarm on my mother's face when a Frenchman winked at her flirtatiously in a café when she was visiting me. When I calmly explained that this cheeky behaviour was not an uncommon occurrence, her look of shock turned to one of discreet pleasure. It is exactly this playful spirit that is part of the Gallic charm, and the French thrive on looking and feeling their best at all times.

The lessons I learned in France unexpectedly, but thankfully, survived my return to Australia. Since leaving France in the early 2000s, marrying an Australian and having two children, I have never deprived myself of any delicious thing. I eat cheese and bread and drink red wine with dinner. I adore chocolate and the regularity with which I eat it is really quite impressive. Yet, even after two pregnancies, I am not overweight or unhealthy. In fact, after converting my Australian husband Simon to the French way of eating, he too has effortlessly lost ten kilos with a smile on his face.

The set of behaviours I learned will help anyone who struggles with losing those last ten kilos, or who repeatedly cycles between overeating and restricting food, or has been exasperated by ever-contradictory nutritional information and simply wants clear, accurate and lasting information on how to eat best. Wherever you were born and currently live and whatever dietary role models you had growing up, the principles of the French diet can be learned and practised by anyone. By understanding why the situation is better in France—where pleasure and gastronomy dominate everyday nutrition—you can see more clearly where you are going wrong. Why do so many people continue to restrict their calorie intake, remove fat and carbohydrates from their diets and exhaust themselves at the gym, only to achieve poor results?

Sadly, fewer and fewer young people are being taught the valuable life skill of simple cooking, as working parents struggle with lack of time and an overload of responsibilities. Learning to enjoy cooking is a serious addition to your health. I have no formal culinary training or revolutionary recipes—only memorable meals fondly savoured around Parisian dinner tables. As I am rather an impatient cook, the recipes I have included here are for 'time-poor' people who want to eat well without spending hours in the kitchen. I call them my short-cut gourmet recipes, because wherever I can cut corners, without compromising the integrity of the finished dish, I do.

As with choosing the right food, learning to check in with your feelings and face them (rather than eat them) is an integral key to losing weight and keeping it off. Excess weight is just a symptom, not the root cause, so learning to identify and address the underlying thoughts and feelings that cause overeating is an integral key to losing weight permanently. I literally lost interest in comfort eating—picking and eating when I wasn't hungry—just by learning to distinguish between true physical hunger and psychological hunger.

Exercise is important for many aspects of our physical and mental health, but you don't have to sweat to be physically fit or religiously punish yourself at the gym. The power of integrated exercise, slotted seamlessly into your daily routine, means that you never need to sign up for a gym membership you won't use much. You can manage your weight while socialising and eating out—these pastimes form an integral part of a fulfilling life and should not be abandoned even when trying to lose weight. There are ways to reward and pamper yourself without consuming unnecessary calories. And as dessert is a subject very dear to me, I suggest ways to have your chocolate and sweets without jeopardising your weight-loss efforts.

You will have your own reasons for wanting to lose weight and put an end to the burden of excess kilos. So every day visualise yourself as a slim person at your natural healthy weight. You may just want to feel great in your own body again, to have more energy for participating in life, to improve your health or to wear the latest fashions. You might have hopes of ending the struggle you have every time you are faced with the foods you love but don't feel entitled to enjoy. Or maybe you are just sick and tired of feeling judged or even ostracised because of your weight.

Like the French, learn to love yourself, flaws and all,

and learn how to spoil yourself thin. If you like the body you live in, you are more likely to like the person who lives there. There is an old Chinese proverb: 'Every journey—great or small—starts with a single step.' Go ahead, be good to yourself, treat yourself well and replenish yourself. The more you listen to your body and love yourself, the better you will be able to achieve your weight-loss goals. This is not about vanity or arrogance—that's not love. It's about having a great respect for yourself and gratitude for your physical body, the only one you were blessed with.

You cannot fail when you learn to trust yourself. Who is the most important person in the world? You are! Relax and enjoy the ride, you fully deserve to be the weight you want to be.

1. Growing Up a Glutton: Learning to Overeat

The Quantity that is sufficient, the Stomach can perfectly concoct and digest, and it will sufficeth the due Nourishment of the Body.
—Benjamin Franklin

Let's start at the beginning—your childhood. In order to understand your current eating habits and why you may struggle to lose weight and keep it off, it is useful to travel back in time and understand how you learned to eat as a child.

The emotional aspect of overeating frequently begins in childhood. As infants, we associate food with love; later it often becomes a substitute for love. As kids we develop eating habits that become automatic behaviour—and we consider these habits perfectly 'normal'. But often a few deeply ingrained negative habits are what prevent us from ever achieving our ideal weight.

Growing up, your role models may routinely have used food as a reward or bribe, to express love, to console or to encourage. As a result, you would have learned that food was synonymous with love, reward, comfort and protection. Conversely, you may have been denied your favourite foods as a form of punishment for bad behaviour. And, like many kids, you may have been forced to finish everything on your plate, even if you didn't like the food or the serving was too large. Some children are not given the opportunity to choose the amount of food that feels comfortable to them.

If there was no or little structure around mealtimes when growing up, you may have unwittingly developed a habit of inhaling your food on the run, in a mad rush, outside of your own awareness—gulping and gobbling, but never really tasting. If you grew up in a large family, with many mouths to feed, you may have even felt threatened that your siblings would pinch your favourite foods from your plate, so you learned to eat with fear and anxiety. Or perhaps your favourite pastime was to munch unconsciously on takeaway or snacks in front of the television—the more interesting the show got, the more you ate, even though you were no longer hungry or even fully aware of your eating. Maybe, out of habit, you regularly ate beyond comfort, because it was expected and therefore felt normal, so that you could squeeze in the dessert you felt you deserved. You may have been told, by well-meaning adults, to 'eat up to get your money's worth' at restaurants, because eating out was a luxury and leaving food on your plate was a sign of disrespect. If such memories sound familiar, don't worry—you are not alone.

Somewhere, somehow, you learned to overeat and not listen to your body. You may have learned to automatically override your body's internal signals of hunger and fullness. Just as you unknowingly took steps to form this pattern, you can take steps to change it. Old eating patterns are easy to continue because they are familiar, even when they're uncomfortable. Yet, with awareness, understanding and, most importantly, action, you can take steps to find the solution you need to achieve balance again.

The 'old me' used to be well acquainted with fullness. As a well-behaved child, I wanted to do the right thing so I ate whatever I was given, whether I was hungry or full, because it got me the praise that I craved. Consequently, I routinely ate plates and plates of praise, and always had room for a little more. You could say my eating style was enthusiastic and random—I never liked to miss a food opportunity.

With food so closely linked with positive associations in my mind, I was also a prime target for the hidden persuaders and incessant marketing constantly at work to get us to eat more than we need. When I hungered for more love and wanted to feel good, I ate. An impressionable young child, I was lured in by the promise of the good times that certain foods could bring. Just like in my favourite television advertisements, I wanted to throw frisbees on the beach in a bikini and eat buckets of deep-fried chicken in the sun. I wanted to experience the euphoria of eating silky chocolate, crunchy nuts and gooey caramel all at once.

The rewards promised by fast and processed foods had a hypnotic effect on me. Eating was synonymous with reward, love, protection, comfort and feeling good. When we unconsciously allow ourselves to react to external cues telling us when, why and how much we should eat, we ignore the inner wisdom we were all born with to regulate our own appetites and weight.

Let me tell you a little about my childhood to illustrate my point. I have always had a passion for food, or more precisely, for eating. You could say my eyes have always been bigger than my stomach, not that I am particularly proud of that fact, because I never wanted to come across as the greedy glutton I secretly was. Yet I used to have trouble ever feeling truly satisfied. Maybe it came from competing with my older brother at mealtimes, gulping down food to see who could finish first. Or perhaps it stems from the fact that growing up with a single working mother, we had to go without a lot of things but there was always plenty of food. Not caviar and smoked salmon, but sweets, biscuits, ice-cream and cakes. My grandmother, who played a significant role in our upbringing, saw weight gain as a sign of maternal success. I adored her because, along with a lot of love and affection, she fed me on a steady diet of sweets, whipping up chocolate malted milkshakes with great flair and passing the well-stocked 'lolly jar' at every opportunity.

On trips to the supermarket with my grandmother, we'd head straight to the confectionary aisle, then grab some milk and ice-cream on the way to the checkout. The fresh fruit and vegetable section inevitably got overlooked. My grandma, proudly chubby and cuddly, was a connoisseur when it came to sweets, but often neglected to think about the main meal. Fish and chips or cheese on toast were common standbys. Preparing healthy, balanced meals was not her forte. A diet of simple carbohydrates was all she knew and she enthusiastically passed it on to her daughter and granddaughter. I grew up understanding that biscuits, cakes and third helpings urged on me were an extension of love, so I learned to eat not only inappropriate portions of the wrong foods but also when I wasn't hungry. No matter how full my stomach was, I always had room for more love. If my mum ever declared that she was on a diet, my grandma would warn her, 'You'll lose your sex appeal!'

My brother and I had no boundaries when it came to food, we filled our cheek pouches to the brim and never learned to slow down or listen to our bodies. It felt normal to be overly full. These eating patterns were passed down unknowingly from generation to generation and left their legacy. My mother, to her credit, tried to enforce better habits, but ultimately, it was a case of monkey see, monkey do.

I saw the way she rewarded herself with a big bag of sweets after a hard day's work. Kids may be deaf, but they're not blind. Mum was also too busy working to keep a careful watch on our nutritional habits.

Upon reflection, I can clearly see why I struggled to find a balanced approach to eating and how the seeds were firmly planted in my early childhood for future struggles with excess weight. When you learn to eat large, large becomes normal. When you acquire the addictive taste for sugar, salt and bad fats early on in life, it is very difficult to get excited about a big green salad or a crunchy apple.

With limited structure around mealtimes and constant grazing on the wrong foods allowed, it was difficult to distinguish between what was real hunger and what was boredom. So I ate not only when I was bored, happy, sad, stressed or depressed, but just because. I ate my fears, my doubts, my past and my future.

Eating was my reliable friend: when life got tough, I knew a packet of cookies was only an arm reach away. I do remember eating fruit, even if it was drowned in castor sugar and accompanied by three scoops of ice-cream. Vegetables were consumed mainly in the form of our national spread Vegemite, or else they were boiled into submission and served water-logged and sadly devoid of crunch and flavour. My brother and I ate them reluctantly, almost with our eyes closed, for one reason only: dessert. Although Mum had good intentions to feed us nutritiously, such meals were not the best training for our tastebuds.

Like most children, I was strongly encouraged to finish everything on my plate, regardless of whether I was full, stuffed or ready to burst—because there were starving people in Ethiopia who could not afford to eat. A big appetite meant that we would grow up to be big and strong. Not only that, but we had to clean our plate or else there was no dessert. So unless I finished everything put in front of me, I believed that somehow I was 'bad' or undeserving.

Consequently, my poor eating habits were deeply ingrained from early on, like a tattoo imprinted on my subconscious. Such habits would lead me into dangerous waters, as I would later discover. Luckily I was a sporty child, so the issue of excess weight did not really hit me until puberty. Then, when I started to be less active and my hormones went crazy, I jumped on the dieting treadmill, desperately trying to rescue myself from those unwanted kilos.

Around this time, when I was fourteen, my mother remarried and our family moved to America to live. I adored America for its excitement and diversity, but I learned to love the hot chocolate fudge sundaes even more.

Although I settled into school quite well, the adjustment was a huge challenge, so I found myself taking solace in the extra large servings dished up at the school cafeteria. It was great to be served a hot lunch of burgers, pizza and fries at midday, when all I had been accustomed to in Australia was stale soggy sandwiches brought from home. The portion sizes were jaw-droppingly impressive and seemed such good value, especially when accompanied by bottomless cups of soft drink. I was truly living in the land of abundance.

We were based in Colorado in winter and my appetite was rather insatiable, due to the extreme cold. Everything in America seemed bigger and better than back home but, alas, it was a disaster for my waistline and did little to help my tendency to overfeed myself.

I had never learned to really listen to my body, or read my true physical hunger, nor did I have the instinct to stop eating when I felt satisfied. Whenever I got homesick, sad and miserable, I would simply whip up another batch of chocolate chip cookies. One of my favourite things to do was to take a trip to the supermarket and buy every new variety of cookies, candy, soft drink and snack food I hadn't tasted before—the novelty being my own form of entertainment. It wasn't until someone bought a movie camera to school to film us acting out a role-play that I suffered my first blow. It was a good seven-to-ten kilo blow straight from left field and hit me like a ton of bricks. I literally didn't recognise myself. I was in a state of shock and denial.

So began a pattern of obsessive dieting. I tried every diet out there: counting calories and/or fat grams, drinking meal replacements and eating protein only.

It was a vicious circle. Every kilo was a struggle to take off and when my resolve weakened, as it inevitably did, the kilos crept back on. I couldn't enjoy treats without guilt and found deprivation depressing. Unsustainable extremism would defeat me in the end, even when I had the best of intentions.

But I was never trying to quit dieting—I was trying to get better at it. Yet the process was chipping away at my self-esteem.

Slowly I began to understand that diets can do more harm than good, especially when they leave you feeling as if you can never quite achieve what you set out to do. I also realised that I was overfeeding myself by eating emotionally in order to dull the hardships of a new family life, a new country, a new school and to cope with the hormonal roller-coaster of going through puberty.

Our twelve-month stay in America was a whirlwind of adventure and excitement, but our family decided to return home to Australia once the school year finished. Although I was excited to come back and see my friends and family, I was apprehensive, knowing that I was not the same size as when I left. I managed to find some clothes that some-what disguised the extra kilos, but deep down I knew that I needed to make fundamental changes to strike a comfortable balance between my love of eating and the care and maintenance of my body and self-esteem.

Being home in Australia somehow restored my equilibrium, yet the fundamental reasons for overeating were still lurking beneath the surface.

My French lessons about how to achieve a sustainable balance between food and lifestyle were yet to come, but I did learn a few things from experiencing a childhood of less-than-perfect role models and from my time spent living in the land of abundance. I call them my 'golden rules'.

GOLDEN RULES

- Just like anything in life, you need boundaries when it comes to food in order to achieve a healthy balance. Eating beyond comfort often stems from an underlying issue or an external cue.

- You are not a 'bad' person if you do not finish everything put in front of you, nor are you impolite if you decline an offer of food. Reclaim the power to be your own judge.

- Take the 'willpower' factor out of the eating equation and start listening to your body's true signals of hunger and satiety. If you are not hungry, then why are you eating?

- Detrimental eating habits ingrained in childhood are simply learned behaviours and can be changed. Our mind and emotions ultimately govern our behaviour, so awareness and understanding are needed before changes can take place.

- Learn to trust your physical hunger, which can be satisfied by a balanced, nutritious meal. Emotional hunger is different and can never be satisfied by food.

- Obsessive dieting sets you up for failure, because restricting food often triggers a primal drive to overeat. If you end up feeling like a failure, ultimately, dieting lowers instead of improves your quality of life.

2. French Impressions

Nothing would be more tiresome than eating and drinking if God had not made them a pleasure as well as a necessity.

—Voltaire

My attraction to France started with the desire to speak another language. I felt the pull of this foreign culture on the other side of the world, a powerful inner need to change and a romantic quest for independence. While attending school in America, I had a wonderful French tutor who captured my imagination and made learning the language exciting for me by teaching me new words from the latest copy of French *Vogue*. I was starting to dream about travelling, and when I finished school Paris seemed much more alluring than the predictable path I was being pressured to follow in Australia. With guidebook in hand and the wide-eyed naïveté of a schoolleaver itching for adventure, I joyously set off solo for an experience as an au pair for a French family in Paris, which would change the course of my life.

I remember stepping off the aeroplane after a marathon 24-hour flight from Australia and discovering Paris for the first time. It was a bit like stepping onto a movie set where familiar monuments I had only seen in books or films suddenly came to life. It is a sophisticated, beautiful and romantic city, with its magnificent buildings, grand boulevards, classy shops and fine food. The only thing that wasn't so classy was trying to dodge the dog poo on the street (fortunately they now pick most of it up). Somehow I managed to walk dog poo right through a high-end boutique one day and I have been traumatised ever since. Embarrassment aside, it felt wonderful to finally be in the City of Light, with so much to see and shop for. French retailers have a flair for presenting everything so exquisitely and seductively and you find you want to buy all manner of things you don't need.

My stay began with being enclosed in a tiny *chambre de bonne* (maid's room) on the top floor of a chic apartment building in the seventh arrondissement (district). The family lived in a grandiose, high-ceilinged apartment over-looking the River Seine. I had secured a job as au pair to a respectable family, both parents of which were doctors. I was to care for their two adorable young boys, who had the most charming accents when they spoke to me in broken English. After I got acquainted with the boys and took *le grand tour* around the apartment, Madame sent me off to my room with a packet of the most divine petit gateaux I had ever tasted.

The routine of getting the boys off to school and meet-ing them when they came home became a bit like Ground-hog Day, but I had plenty of free time during the day and in the evenings to explore Paris. For me this meant eating my way from patisserie to patisserie, trying to decide once and for all where they made the best *tarte au citron*, a tangy, velvety slice of heaven which seemed to slide effortlessly down my throat.

In Paris, the perfumes of food escape and waft through open doorways, lingering seductively on the streets. Like an animal hunting, my deep and abiding concern for the stomach led me to discover an endless array of edible de-lights. Part of working as an au pair was the understand-ing that I would naturally attend French classes at the lo-cal language school. But I soon realised I could get better verbal practice ordering three courses from le menu at the local brasserie than I ever got in the classroom. When it came to food, I knew how to make myself understood. So I spent many happy afternoons practising my second language with seductive French waiters as I polished off my favourite dishes.

How I loved this bustling city, the underground world of the metro, the bouncy bus rides along cobbled streets, the charm and elegance of the tree-lined Avenue Champs-Elysees, stopping often to eat warm nutella-filled crepes in quaint cafés. After school, the children somehow managed to amuse themselves in the confines of the apartment, albeit one with a stunning view—a routine that seemed so far removed from the liberty and space of my own childhood.

With no real childcare skills apart from those derived from weekend babysitting jobs in Australia, I embraced my responsibility seriously. I had no useful cooking talents either, yet this bourgeois Parisian family sparked in me an uncontrollable fascination with mealtimes. I began to taste and experience foods I had never come across, such as artichokes with vinaigrette dressing. I became fascinated by the practice of sensuously sucking each leaf of its goodness until I reached the much sought-after heart and devouring it triumphantly. Similarly, I never dreamed that mussels simmered in white wine and herbs could be so delicious or that raw fennel bulbs sliced and served au naturel would be so refreshing and intensely flavourful.

As au pair I became a member of the family, dining en famille every evening, sharing lively conversation and what I considered to be excellent food. Visits to the fresh food *marche* (street market) with Madame became a much anticipated highlight of my week, where we carefully selected ripe seasonal produce — fruits, vegetables, meat, poultry and pungent, aromatic cheeses. This is when I really discovered the joys of market shopping and the wonders of la salade, a green leafy mix served with a tangy vinaigrette dressing. I never dreamed something so good for you could taste so delicious.

Evening meals in the Paris household were light, luscious and civilised. The table was attractively set, the television turned off and all thoughts and attention were focused on the joys of the food and the company. We would enjoy simple healthy combinations such as ratatouille and sautéed white fish or chicken with herbs de provence, followed by a leafy green salad, red wine, baguette and cheese, finished off with a natural yoghurt or fruit. I discovered that the French eat quite simply and lightly at home, but each meal is balanced and delicious. Contrary to popular belief, they don't wallow in butter, cream, pork, cheeses, goose fat and sausages at every meal or guzzle wine like fish. Croissants for breakfast are more of a weekly treat than a daily staple.

Surprisingly, what struck me most was the fact that there were practically no fat people in Paris. It was mind boggling to me that an abnormally high percentage of French men and women have the fabulous bodies that make fashion into a statement without ever having sweated through a step class. I never once saw Madame take formal exercise and yet she had a model figure, even after giving birth to two children. What exactly was the 'secret' I was missing?

The household pantry was certainly well stocked with good things to eat and even though I enjoyed three meals a day with the family, I was still often on the prowl in their pantry for something to satisfy a deeper craving. It never occurred to me that I could actually be homesick and that no amount of nutella or Häagen-Dazs ice-cream was going to cure it. One day, Monsieur, suave and distinguished, discreetly pulled me aside and expressed concern over how much I was eating. I remember not only feeling embarrassed but also insecure about my eating behaviour, because I had no idea why I lacked willpower. He said he didn't care if entire packets of biscuits went missing, he was just concerned about my wellbeing. Given that he was a specialist surgeon, I gathered he knew what he was talking about. Nevertheless, at that point I lacked the necessary insight to address the underlying thoughts and feelings that caused me to overeat.

As my first sojourn in Paris came to an end, I realised that I had developed a true passion for food. It was this initial French experience that led me to want to change my eating habits for good. The horizons of my palate had been opened up and I now knew that eating good food meant learning to plan ahead to shop, prepare and cook to make each meal special.

By immersing myself in French culture and observing their traditions close at hand, I had began to look at food in a new light. Mealtimes were an event to be eagerly embraced and treasured, rather than a mental struggle of guilty feelings. I was thoroughly fascinated with this new attitude, but I was still like an outsider looking in, knowing instinctively that the French eating habits made a lot of sense, yet still struggling to actually change my old ways.

Three meals a day, not counting the children's obligatory after-school snack of baguette and dark bitter chocolate, ceremoniously laying the table, washing and drying the salad leaves, bringing the cheese to room temperature and preparing the fruit bowl became a source of great pleasure and an essential part of my Parisian life. Sitting down to a lengthy session of self-indulgence, savouring a variety of flavours, peppered with lively discussion, laughter and love, I began to understand the power of food.

It was this structured routine, three times a day, involving more care and respect about what I chose to eat that unexpectedly survived my return to life back in Australia. As I defiantly attempted to shun the temptations of solitary snacking and the table-less culture of life back home, I found myself yearning for the influential memory of my first French family.

Upon my return home to Melbourne, I enrolled to study at beauty therapy college, to become what in France is known as an *esthéticienne* — I had grown up around the world of beauty, with my mum being a hairdressing and beauty teacher. As a child I had fond memories of helping my mother with clients on Saturdays when she worked from home. My Parisian experience had sparked an even greater fascination with personal grooming and the world of beauty, glamour, sophistication and pampering. It seemed like a natural path to follow, as I had quickly adopted the same attitude to the pursuit of beauty as French women have. We've all heard the slogan 'because you're worth it'. The French, in particular, seem to get this. They consider personal grooming an adult responsibility, rather than a self-indulgent pastime.

They understand how to spoil themselves with a new scarf, a dress or a perfume. This pursuit of pleasure, coupled with a healthy level of self-respect, has a ripple effect that carries over to what they choose to eat, which explains why they will not settle for mediocre food. It is not selfish to take care of yourself, in fact it is one of the most important things you can do for yourself and for your family. The French learn from their mothers to plan ahead and anticipate their meals. When you feel good about your relationship with food, you automatically discard unsatisfying eating situations and un-appealing foods. When you give yourself the freedom to eat what you love without guilt, you are sending yourself a message of not only love, but of trust and self-respect.

My first trip to Paris left a lasting impression, particularly when it came to the difference in dietary habits compared with what I had grown up with. I realised the French have a low obesity rate, not because they are genetically blessed, but quite simply due to their balanced approach to food and eating, combined with the moderate and sustainable approach of integrating exercise into their daily life.

Eating beyond comfort, to cope with life or to tranquilise yourself is, for the French, the equivalent of pure body abuse. They prefer to stay in the pleasure and awareness zones when it comes to eating. Generally speaking, they don't go in for crazy diet extremes because they instinctively understand that resistance to food is futile. If you allow yourself a little bit now, it saves eating a whole lot later on! No foods need to be forbidden if you can manage balanced amounts. Therefore, the French just don't have that all-or-nothing approach to eating. Perfection is not possible, nor is it necessary.

Many people draw their lives boldly in black and white, with no grey areas. When it comes to eating, they either eat perfectly, or they fail. Often, they fail. But such an approach actually sets them up for failure because none of us can succeed forever in eating perfectly, nor should we try. Compared with other cultures, the French eat less and enjoy it more because they give eating their full attention and don't view each meal as a win or lose experience. A whole day is not ruined by a side order of fries or a chocolate bar. When they do eat heavier foods, they get great pleasure and find it easy to stop at satisfaction. For the most part, they naturally have a more integrated approach, walk more, watch less television and structure their eating habits around a routine that brings pleasure to their daily life.

On this first trip to Paris, I was simply an observer, clinging to the deeply embedded, mindless eating habits I had grown up with. As I watched the French with fascination and admiration, I nevertheless continued to snack mindlessly, eat on the run, overindulge in fast foods and eat with my emotions rather than by listening to my body. Yet I was beginning to see the light.

I returned to Australia with my surplus ten kilos firmly intact. It is one thing to observe a great example, yet it is somewhat more challenging to actually change one's mindset and implement a brand new path of behaviours. Understanding and awareness are necessary steps towards changing behaviour, but the most important one is action. If you want results, you have to take small steps to permanently change.

Many of my Australian friends interrogated me about how the French stay so slim while eating croissants and camembert. Although it had clearly not yet worked for me, my response was that the French instinctively understand what the appropriate portion size is. They prioritise shopping, preparing and cooking good food, choose quality over quantity and rarely feel the need to snack in between three balanced, nutritious meals a day. On top of this, they engage in lots of exercise in the form of walking, stair climbing (and horizontal jogging!). They do drink alcohol, but rarely get drunk. And of course they eat small amounts of wonderfully rich foods, but never to the point of having to loosen their belts.

You can learn so much from good role models — here are my initial observations from my first stay in France.

GOLDEN RULES
- The French eating habits revolve around a structured routine, prioritising balance, moderation and

variety. This includes plenty of vegetables, fruit, soups and salads, quality protein, good fats and dairy products. And a little wine, cheese, chocolate and dessert.

- The French are less inclined to use food as a coping mechanism when life gets tough. They don't take their emotions out on a plate of pastries.
- The French eat at home more often than at restaurants and cook simple, tasty meals from scratch.
- Portion sizes are smaller compared with other countries (in Paris the size of a croissant is half that of one in Colorado; even the individual yoghurts sold in France are 25 per cent smaller than those in Australia).
- Eating is a social activity. The French serve several small dishes and eat them slowly and mindfully, with plenty of time between courses for the physiological feedback of satiety to kick in. The cheese course, for example, would be the size of two dice, not an entire wheel of brie!
- The French hardly ever snack outside of meals. They believe that food tastes better when you are hungry and great meals are worth waiting for.
- Good quality cheese, dark bitter chocolate and red wine are savoured in moderation.
- Food is at the forefront of the daily routine, rather than an afterthought tucked in between all other responsibilities.

✜

LES SALADES

French families prefer simple salads as a second course and larger, more complex salads as a main course for dinners at home. Try making your own salads by using a mixed green-leaf salad tossed in vinaigrette as the base.

SIMPLE VINAIGRETTE

Simple vinaigrette is so easy to make and once you have tried it, you will be eternally convinced of the refreshing, palette-cleansing properties of a pure, unadulterated salad. It can be prepared in minutes. The most successful uses Dijon mustard, mixed with some red wine vinegar and then blended with a combination of olive oil and vegetable oil, seasoned with salt and pepper and then whisked to a homogeneous sauce. It is ready to be shaken and enjoyed, tossed with a mixed green-leaf salad. It is also wonderful poured over blanched asparagus or steamed green beans.

SALAD NIÇOISE

Chop some tomatoes and arrange them over the salad greens, place a mound of tuna in the centre, with some quartered hardboiled eggs around the tuna. Add a handful of tasty, black Niçoise style olives and sprinkle the salad with some *herbes de provence* (you can make your own by mixing dried herbs such as basil, thyme, rosemary, tarragon, summer savory, fennel seeds and marjoram) and extra vinaigrette if needed. Anchovy fillets, boiled baby potatoes and blanched green beans are additional options if you desire.

WARM GOAT'S CHEESE SALAD

To make croutons, slice some day-old baguette into 3cm (1in) rounds and toast. Meanwhile, dress the salad leaves in vinaigrette and place on serving plate. Place rounds of goat's cheese on top of the croutons and heat under the grill until bubbling. Arrange the bubbling croutons on top of the dressed leaves and serve.

SMOKED TROUT AND GREEN OLIVE SALAD

Flake a fillet of smoked trout over a bed of dressed green leaves. Top with some marinated split green olives and serve with crusty bread. You can find marinated green olives in good delicatessens or at your local market.

CHICKEN ADVOCADO SALAD

You can poach or sauté a chicken breast, but it is also a great way to use up any leftover chicken. Shred the chicken over a bed of dressed leaves and slice a small, ripe avocado over the chicken. Season with salt and pepper and top with fresh parsley and a touch more vinaigrette.

TOMATO AND MOZZARELLA SALAD

This is a favourite of mine. It can be prepared in minutes and enjoyed as a meal in itself. Instead of starting with a bed of leafy greens, slice large rounds of ruby red, vine-ripened tomatoes and arrange them on a plate. Thinly slice balls of fresh buffalo mozzarella and place on top of the tomatoes. Pour over the vinaigrette and dress with shredded basil leaves. Enjoy it with crusty bread.

ROQUEFORT AND WALNUT SALAD

Add cubes of Roquefort cheese to a bed of dressed mixed green leaves, and then sprinkle with crushed walnuts.

SALADE COMPOSE

Toss some green mixed lettuce leaves in simple vinaigrette. Meanwhile, boil 4 eggs until just firm, then peel and cut into quarters. To make croutons, cut 8 slices of baguette 1cm (½in) thick and lightly toast. Fry 4 thick bacon rashes and drain on absorbent paper. Add the eggs, crumbled bacon and croutons to the salad leaves and top with a drizzle of olive oil.

3. Adopting the French Way

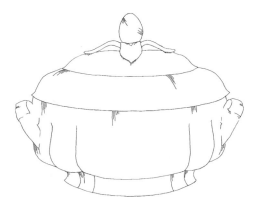

We should look for someone to eat and drink with before looking for something to eat and drink.

—Epicurus

When I came back to Australia, naturally I wanted to recreate the wonderful memories of the mealtimes I had come to love with my Parisian family. With the best of intentions, I started to convert my family to the French tradition, setting the table with napkins, candles and wine glasses, slicing fresh baguettes to accompany the meal, whipping up a sharp mustard vinaigrette for *la salade*, pureeing big pots of vegetable soup and shopping at the market for fresh fish, poultry, fruit, vegetables and aromatic cheeses.

In Paris I had learned that the beauty of the dining table—the choice of plates, cutlery and glassware—can go a long way to satisfying our hunger for beauty. To make something memorable, it must look appealing—ripe seasonal fruit, beautifully cut and presented on a fine china platter, for instance. Even drinking sparkling water, with a fresh lemon wedge or sprig of mint in an attractive glass, will make you feel like 'you're worth it'.

Fine dining restaurants invest a lot of thought and energy in getting their presentation and décor just right. You can do the same for yourself and your family at home every day. Are you saving those beautiful plates and glasses for a day that never seems to come? Start spoiling yourself, as you would an honoured guest. The dining atmosphere can enhance the eating experience, so that we leave the table satisfied and nourished on more levels than just the physical one.

Back in Melbourne, preparing these precious meals became the best cookery classes for me—I became a recipe book addict and novice cook, having no homely parental advice or culinary secrets to draw on. Even now, when planning a meal, I try to visualise how the food will look on the plate in order to achieve balance and beauty. Colour and textural contrasts are as important as flavour variations. I love simplicity and I love the vibrancy of red and yellow capsicum, as well as the deep orange of sweet potato and pumpkin for their ability to jazz up a meal, and I always serve a green vegetable. When you serve fresh asparagus with a simple vinaigrette or strawberries with a dollop of real cream, you don't have to apologise for the simplicity. Nature is on your side.

Turning off the television at mealtimes and initiating conversation about the day's activities took my family somewhat by surprise, but they were hugely appreciative of my newfound enthusiasm and efforts. In their minds, my sojourn in Paris had changed me from a mindless munching glutton to more of a gourmet, a word for someone who adores food, eats it with discernment and refinement and savours every morsel that goes into their mouth. As a family we actually talked more, slowed down our eating, relaxed, and savoured the simply prepared meals. I was admittedly no Michelin star chef, but definitely an enthusiastic home cook. I now believed fine dining and an appreciation of the better things in life could be a regular feature of any household, wherever you live. It just took planning ahead, rather than opting to eat whatever was around. Gone was the insatiable need for processed snacks on the go, constant grazing and the table-less culture we had become accustomed to in Australia. Mealtimes *à la français* were now worth waiting for. Prioritising balanced meals was definitely a step in the right direction, but I still struggled with knowing when to stop eating.

Then I met a Frenchman from Paris, Frederic, who was living in Australia, and we hit it off immediately. At last I had someone to practise speaking French with and share my yearning for life back in the City of Love (Paris has several such names). Although I had experienced a good dose of French culture, I was still far from being a slim and chic Parisienne. It seems I had other qualities that intrigued Frederic—yet, in his charming but very blunt Gallic way, he made it clear to me one day that I could do with slimming down.

Obviously Frederic thought I ate too much and didn't know when to stop (which was a very accurate observation). I didn't quite know how to swallow this blatant comment, but I did have enough understanding of French culture to know that this sort of brutal honesty is how loved ones speak to each other in France. They don't hold back when it comes to saying how it is. Rather than whisper behind your back, the French will say it to your face. He was astonished that I often ate more than he did, and became agitated when I constantly asked, Hey, are you going to finish that?' To add fuel to the fire, he could clearly see that I had no 'brakes' when it came to eating sweets! '*Un désastre,*' he declared profoundly. I shrugged off what I knew, deep down, to be the truth. Sometimes, though, it is easier to hear the truth. Realising that I needed help was, oddly enough, a relief. I knew I had to take action and solve my weight problem once and for all. It wasn't just about what I was eating, it was also about getting to the bottom of what was eating me.

As my studies in Australia were near finishing, I decided to take the opportunity to spend three months in America as part of a student work visa program. I was looking forward to my American trip and was not going to let anyone persuade me not to go, not even a blossoming romance with a suave, handsome Frenchman.

So I set off on my own for the exciting and thrilling land of abundance once again. As I got settled and found a job working in a beauty salon in fun-filled Las Vegas, again I fell into the golden arches—that old burger-fries-soda trap—snacking 24/7. Devouring moist, oversized buttery muffins washed down with large syrupy coffees at the local Starbucks became a daily occurrence. I began grabbing takeaway fast food and inhaling my meals on the run, then visiting the drugstore, which stocked an enormous variety of highly processed snack foods just in case I got hungry later on.

My good intentions about eating to honour my health and waistline quickly flew out the window. I made excuses to justify my chaotic approach to eating. Without a car, getting to a fresh food market proved difficult and my motivation to shop and prepare healthy meals quickly dwindled. Convenience and instant gratification were just too tempting and before I knew it my jeans weren't fitting any more.

It was around this time that I got a call from Frederic saying he wanted to come and see me in America. I was surprised, but flattered that he would fly such a distance to see me. 'Sure,' I replied with enthusiasm, 'come on over.' This was followed by a sudden rush of panic as I remembered the state of my expanding backside. When I collected Frederic at the airport, I distinctly remember he looked quite stunned. I could see what he was thinking, although in those first few moments, he said nothing—it must have taken all the French restraint he could muster. But we both knew the truth: I was getting fatter!

Frederic and I had a wonderful time, even though he did have me gasping for breath, jogging up and down the Strip every morning. I enjoyed showing him the all-you-can-eat buffets served at many of the grand hotels. I thought he would be particularly charmed by the Paris Hotel, with its mini Eiffel Tower and Arc De Triomphe. Surely the French-style buffet offered at the hotel would tickle this Parisian, I thought. But the concept of eating yourself silly for a flat fee left him with a confused and crumpled expression on his furrowed brow. He clearly did not share my enthusiasm for the opportunity to eat until your tummy hurt. For a Frenchman, the all-you-can-eat concept seemed like an absurd idea.

We decided we would move to Paris to be together once my stay in America ended. In Las Vegas, I actually did not feel so fat because most people around me were much, much fatter. But the zipper on my jeans did not lie. I knew I needed to make permanent changes to my eating habits if I wanted to feel good about myself in the long term.

It was no surprise to my family back home that I had developed wanderlust. When I moved back to Paris with Frederic we were warmly welcomed into his traditional family household. His mother Josianne, my adopted French mother as I affectionately called her, was thrilled that her son had finally bought a girl home to meet her. We enjoyed an instant rapport and Josianne, petite and glamorous with an infectious laugh, was to become my charming mentor and confidante when it came to really understanding and grasping the mysteries of the 'French paradox'.

By watching her closely, how she shopped and cooked on a daily basis (even with a full-time job), I learned precisely how the French appear to have their cake and eat it too—how they stay svelte without ever setting foot inside a gym. Finally I had someone who confided in me like a daughter, coaching me on my way to a fabulous figure. I was so curious to get to the bottom of what most French people do without a second thought. I wanted to really learn their well-honed tricks and prove that a willing, non-French student could be made thin for the rest of her life, just by doing as the French do.

Sure, I knew what a balanced meal looked like, I had ample exercise throughout the day and I felt I should have my eating 'sorted out' by now. But I believed that genetics—ie, my metabolism—were not on my side, and I was beginning to give up on managing my weight. I was ready to accept I was born to be heavy. After all, the more I tried to control my insatiable appetite and weight, the more I struggled to achieve the necessary balance. Yet, as I immersed myself into life chez Josianne and picked her brains in my less-than-perfect French, I slowly began to understand where I had been going wrong.

As eating is a big part of French *joie de vivre*, deprivation is not on the menu, nor is eliminating entire food groups or religiously counting calories or fat grams. The attitude to eating is not boldly painted in black and white with rigid rules and no room to move. Sure, they stick to a regular eating routine. But within the context of a meal, enjoyment and satisfaction are the priorities. They eat at mealtimes and when they've finished, they go about their day. They are naturally guided by their internal cues of hunger and satiety and prefer to stay in the pleasure zone with food. That means they serve and eat smaller portions and feel satisfied with less food. Stuffing themselves beyond comfort doesn't harmonise with the pursuit of pleasure.

Unlike in many other cultures, the joy of eating is still alive and well in France—the pleasures that food brings have not been tainted by fear and worry. For years, I had been conditioned to think that food was either good or bad, could make you sick or make you fat, therefore much of the joy of eating for me had been taken away. Ironically, this fear and resistance often backfired on me, and I ate more, just in case it was the last time I was ever going to allow myself the pleasure. Years of dieting meant that I had trained myself to ignore and override the signals of my body in order to fit in with the eating guidelines of the latest diet I was on. Consequently, I didn't trust my body or my food choices and certainly didn't feel like I deserved to eat what I really loved, because I might not want to stop. It was a vicious circle.

In Paris this second time, I really began to change my thoughts about dieting. In the end I turned away from dieting, which seemed a little scary at first, but I figured it had clearly never worked for me anyway. After all, I thought, if I just followed the eating habits of my adopted French family—who were all enviably lean—surely I couldn't go wrong. If they didn't need to snack incessantly, then I didn't need to either. When I sat down to the family meals, I felt real physical hunger, a feeling I had long ago forgotten and suppressed. It's when I finally realised that hunger really is the best seasoning.

With the guidance of my French family, I felt relieved to learn that it was perfectly normal to desire and consume creamy cheeses, rich chocolate, red wine and crusty bread, because such foods, eaten in appropriate portion sizes within the context of a balanced meal, will not make you fat. In fact, energy-dense foods like these will leave you satisfied after only small amounts, if you eat them slowly and with your full attention. A desire to eat the foods you love is not seen as a weakness of character among the French, as life without great food would be very dull. Eating is more like a ritual of self-pampering and a daily hedonistic ambition than an afterthought slotted quickly and hurriedly into the day's responsibilities.

When you have self-respect, as the French do, you learn to plan your meals ahead and have the discipline to follow through with your decisions. You can't expect to eat well if you don't think about your meal and shop in advance.

If you wait until you are overly hungry and then grab the nearest thing you can get your hands on, you are more likely to reach for poor quality food. A big part of being slim is having a routine that makes eating the right things a habit, rather than a battle.

True, the French give themselves permission to regularly eat foods that would make a professional dieter's bottom lip quiver—full-fat cheese, croissants, chocolate, butter and real cream—but they do so mindfully and in small amounts. Most French women and men, therefore, have maintaining a stable weight down to a fine art. The key point is that when you give yourself permission to eat, you begin to eat what you like best, rather than what you think you 'should'. Eating what you truly love, when you are genuinely hungry, means that you are more easily able to stop eating once you're satisfied. Eating the low-calorie equivalent often just doesn't measure up to the real thing.

It is interesting to note that if you eat what you don't really like, when you're not really hungry (according to some rule book), you will often continue to be on the prowl for more food to satisfy yourself. Eventually you will get around to eating what you really wanted in the first place. When you give yourself the liberty to make your own food choices, and back it up with trust in your own decisions, you begin to let go of that 'last supper' mentality, because you know you can eat your favourite foods again when you are hungry. In my experience of caring for their babies and children, French mothers are not overly forceful in insisting the kids finish every last morsel of food. Instead they expose the children to good food and give them the freedom to develop their personal preferences—they are allowed to eat the amount that feels right to them, so they are guided by their internal cues of hunger and fullness.

The French understand that complete deprivation is somewhat futile. Their day is not ruined by a piece of birthday cake or a serve of crème brulee. Instead, they eat without guilt, eat real food (not diet foods) and therefore find it easy to stop when they no longer feel hungry. They eat what they want, but never more than they need. After all, there is never any reason to overeat now, when you know you can eat it again later, when you're hungry.

When you give yourself permission to eat what really pleases you and pay attention to how different foods make your body feel after eating, surprisingly you naturally lean towards foods that nourish our bodies and honour our health. Fresh, wholesome foods contain the vitamins, minerals and energy we need to live a vibrant life. A life full of junky food can really sap your energy. The French gastronome Anthelme Brillat-Savarin said, 'Tell me what you eat and I will tell you what you are.' Choose great, fresh food and notice how good you feel.

According to Josianne, self-respect and feeling good about yourself, as well as learning to trust the needs and wants of your body, are very useful if you want to fight the flab—the French know how to love themselves, flaws and all. This attitude means they look after themselves, just as much as they care for their families. If our primary objective when eating is to feel good, then staying attuned and responsive to our inner satiety cues is crucial. There is never a legitimate reason to eat beyond comfort because, according to Josianne, eating until you're stuffed is the equivalent of self-sabotage. Similarly, when drinking alcohol for the pleasure of it, there is never a good reason to drink like a fish.

When you eat from a mindset of abundance, rather than scarcity or restriction, you begin to understand that there is no reason to eat it all now, when you know you can eat it again later.

In fact, food tastes best when you are actually hungry, so the French are used to welcoming the feeling of hunger before they sit down to eat, rather than fearing it. Sometimes we eat when we are not hungry too. When I expressed concern about my overpowering PMS cravings, I was quite relieved when Josianne said that surrendering to occasional food cravings, within reason, is a sensible practice rather than a weakness and will not make you fat. Trying to resist what you are really craving in the midst of full-blown PMS symptoms can actually backfire by producing a primal drive to overeat. In other words, treating a little now, saves regretting a whole lot later on!

While on the subject of women's issues, Josianne also subtly suggested a wardrobe makeover. So I realised it was time to ditch the loose-fitting, baggy, elasticised-waisted clothing and find some well-cut things that emphasised my waist better (I have a typical hourglass shape) and did up with a zipper and button, which would help keep me in check. Unconsciously, because of my fluctuating weight, I had fallen into the habit of buying clothes a little too big. Alas, with reliable French honesty, Josianne suggested I started buying things that fitted, rather than hide behind clothes that were too baggy. Rather than wait until I lost weight to buy new clothes, I packed away anything that didn't fit and set about finding my own style and some new clothes. As with most Frenchmen, Frederic was on hand to help me select my new wardrobe and help me to work out what really suited my figure.

Shopping for clothes in Paris is hardly a chore. In fact, it's every fashionista's dream because you really are spoiled for choice. Although my budget didn't stretch far enough to reach the designer boutiques of Rue St Honore, I still managed to spoil myself without sending myself under. Previously I had shied away from changing rooms and trying on clothes, but I soon developed an appreciation of how important it is to try things on and how the right cut can enhance the overall silhouette of your figure.

To me, it was an important step to start wearing clothes that I felt great in, with pieces that flatter and fit properly. As Frederic pointed out, dowdy clothes make you eat more than you really need to. As I lost weight, I could measure my success by how my clothes fitted, which made me feel good. It wasn't about squeezing into an impossibly small size, but by weaning myself off the baggy jeans, loose sweaters and track pants, I became more aware of my body. By making more effort to dress with a flattering fit, I naturally gave myself a morale boost that encouraged weight loss and more conscious eating choices.

The more I got to know my French friends, the more I began to understand that the key to loving yourself more is first accepting yourself and your uniqueness. The French are more seduced by charm and character than by perfection. Attractiveness comes from intelligence, confidence, wit and a sense of humour. And there is an art to emphasising your positive attributes and camouflaging what you like less. I began to realise that, regardless of the current fashion, I was never going to look real good in a mini skirt, but I learned to dress around that. By comparing yourself with unrealistic media images and counting all the ways you feel you fall short, you miss out on your own beauty. We all come in different body shapes and sizes that we cannot control, such as height, bone structure and density. But being uncomfortably overweight is a factor we can control and we certainly do not need to accept as our fate.

The French appear to refuse to accept or even see themselves as being overweight. They don't give up on themselves. They don't use excuses. I can't speak for the whole of France, but in my experience they are more likely to address underlying issues and inbalances before they get out of control. It seems they have been using the 'law of attraction' for many years: we are all a product of what we think about most often, and they only think of themselves as thin! Knowing what a good portion size is (knowing, for instance, that a serve of steak, rice or pasta should be no bigger than the palm of your hand) and incorporating lots of physical movement into one's day are key factors in staying eternally slim for life. They also stick to a regular eating routine, which ensures structure rather than chaos. It's traditional, but it's also a safeguard against mindless eating.

Josianne never set foot inside a gym, and I don't think she even owned a pair of running shoes. But every morning she slipped into her high heels and marched out the door with great purpose. Her physical day was an obstacle course of walking up hills, climbing stairs, leaping on and off the metro, dodging the crowds along lengthy underground corridors and lots of walking while she crisscrossed Paris on foot. When she came home at night, she barely stopped moving until bedtime. As she was petite, she was always in heels—even her slippers had heels. I don't know how she did it, but she did have great calves. It was just what she did and, after all, in a society that thrives on the art of personal allure, wearing heels made her feel good. Feeling good in your clothes (and sexy lingerie) is a constant reminder to make choices that pay off in slimness.

According to Josianne, a big part of being slim is what she likened to a mental 'priority list' of indulgences worth having—meaning you should have what you truly desire, but in small portions and at carefully chosen moments. It's like bargaining with yourself, so that you feel good about your treats and eat them without guilt. This way, you can fully appreciate and savour your indulgences when you choose to, but are still able to balance everything out over a whole day or week. This requires thinking and planning ahead. If you can plan for and anticipate a party or a special occasion, you are better able to make allowances to cancel out your discrepancies. More importantly, by giving yourself permission to indulge, you no longer experience feelings of deprivation which, as mentioned, can be a real impediment to successful weight loss.

Believe it or not, in France, I learned to get more joy and satisfaction from a small piece of rich, dark chocolate than I ever got from an entire family block before. When you start to give yourself permission to eat without guilt, there is no reason to devour the whole lot in one foul swoop. I have a real ritual now for eating chocolate: I usually eat it with a cup of warm tea so that it slowly melts on my tongue and I can fully appreciate the silky texture, rich flavour and subtle notes and aroma. The experience is truly one of life's great pleasures and I vow never to abstain—not for any diet. Neither do you have to.

I now believe you don't have to give up chocolate to be slim and healthy—not if you learn to manage the art of moderate consumption. If you can't keep it in the house to begin with—even to give yourself time to learn to trust yourself with it—then don't. Instead, venture out occasionally and buy it in very small quantities to enjoy fully. Even if it is just a small square of dark chocolate, sit down and let it linger sensuously in your mouth, allow the different notes of cocoa to dissolve on your tongue and slide slowly down your throat, stimulating your tastebuds fully. Amazingly, you will find that a very small portion, when eaten this way, can have a big impact on your satisfaction levels. It's a bit different from shovelling down a bag of M&Ms, hunched over a computer, while you concentrate intently on your work rather than on the pleasure of the chocolate. By allowing yourself small amounts when you really want it, soon you will find it has lost its magnetic power over you. Ultimately, you will learn to enjoy small amounts in the context of a balanced diet.

The French have a saying, 'We taste first with our eyes'. What I love is that beauty has no calories and yet it improves our overall wellbeing. When preparing food, you need to create a feast for the eyes, 'to fool the stomach', making a little bit seem like a lot. The more you plan your meals, the less tempted you will be to overdo in quantity. Never underestimate the power of presentation when it comes to food. Creating attractive meals is a great artistic opportunity, a chance to nurture your desire for a creative outlet. It appeals to your aesthetic sense and makes you feel special. An elegant presentation can even make you believe the food tastes better. Making the effort to present your food attractively is a powerful way to enjoy it more. A thinly sliced banana, fanned delicately on a dessert plate, drizzled with a little honey, sprinkled with cinnamon and eaten with a small fork is a stark contrast to wolfing down a banana in two gulps in front of the TV. If you want to live a beautiful life, you have to make the effort to create meaningful ceremonies with our food.

If you pay attention, you will realise that all your senses come to a peak in the ritual of eating. When you hear the crunch of an apple, smell the aroma of fresh coffee, feel the velvety texture of avocado on your tongue and get relief from an icy cold sorbet on a hot summer's day, you are engaging all your senses. When you garnish a melon with a sprig of fresh mint, you are sending a message to yourself that you are worth the extra effort it takes — and showing you also appreciate those around you. In essence, your attitude towards food and eating is often a reflection of how you feel about yourself and your life. Needless to say, restrictive dieting sends unconscious messages of fear and shortage and your body and mind react accordingly. The process of dieting, or artificial famine, actually lowers instead of improves your quality of life. Isn't it far better to start eating in a way that you can comfortably maintain for the rest of your life? When you eat balanced meals, in a way that pleases your tastebuds and honours your health, with variety and moderation, you are guaranteed to feel much better.

Achieving the necessary balance with food and drink is not about viewing yourself as a success or a failure with each day or each meal. Try not to criticise yourself, as there is no failure in learning. The mindset needed to achieve a healthy weight for life begins with patience. The idea is not to drop weight in time for a special event or holiday, the aim is to learn to listen to your body and let it be your guide to achieving a healthy weight for life. Just as life is not always black or white, eating is not an all or nothing scenario.

There are no forbidden foods if you can manage your portions. More often it is the mindless and non-hunger eating that creates weight gain. You may already eat very well at mealtimes, but it is the stress or emotional eating in between that defeats you.

We are all human—sometimes circumstances mean that you will overindulge or eat when you are not physically hungry. But if you do so with conscious awareness and with a view to compensate later on, it balances out nicely. It doesn't mean you should beat yourself up if you have a piece of birthday cake at the office party and enjoy every last mouthful. But if you find yourself going back for seconds or thirds, you need to make a plan. Perhaps aim to take a ten-minute walk in the fresh air after one piece of cake, and return to the office feeling optimistic rather than regretful. Like the French, allow yourself to enjoy the eating experience, the celebration of life's special moments, without the guilt.

As a rough guide, 90 per cent of the time, try eating more consciously than you are used to (your intuition knows instinctively what the best nutritional choices are). Think fresh, ripe and seasonal. Just try to do better than you normally do. Choose food that comes from farmers, rather than factories.

Save the 10 per cent for special occasions, when you want to really let your hair down. The French base their daily diets on whatever the season is offering, but they also know how to treat themselves. You can make a first-class meal with everyday ingredients that are ripe and well selected.

Go ahead, touch and smell the fruit and vegetables before buying—it's part of the tactile fun of shopping for food. By touching and smelling, you will get to know when a melon is ripe and ready and when a pineapple is at its sweetest. By using your senses, you become a better shopper.

Typically at home the French serve lots of homemade soups, salads, vegetables, fruit, fish, lean meat and poultry. Most rich desserts, sauces, pastries and charcuterie are more occasional treats, rather than everyday staples. Fresh baguettes—really fresh—are certainly eaten daily, but croissants are more of a once a week treat, if that.

There is a satisfying way to live and eat well even with budget constraints—that is, be selective about what you buy so as to minimise waste. By making meals from scratch, you can avoid the highly processed, chemical-laden, packaged foods containing highly addictive substances, such as high fructose corn syrup, artificial sweeteners and monosodium glutamate. Often packaged and processed foods are not only of questionable quality, but they cost more too. They rob your health and your hip pocket. The French don't favour foods that have been stripped of their natural goodness and replaced with something artificial. Refreshingly, they believe that what nature has to offer is a lot more appealing—and ultimately more satisfying.

Compared with those in other countries, French supermarkets offer very little in the way of low-fat and fat-free products. This is because the French would rather consume the real flavour of full fat, but in small amounts. In any case, the problem with these products is the false impression that 'fat-free' means a licence to eat double or triple the quantity, which still makes you fat. Most of the time, 'diet foods' fail dismally in the satisfaction department, and before too long you are on the prowl for something that will really hit the spot.

A big reason low-fat eating has failed to improve our waistlines is that the decrease in fat comes hand-in-hand with an increase in sugar consumption. If you're in the business of selling cookies and you've taken the fat out, you still have to make them taste great—and cheaply. So the fat is replaced with more sugars, such as high-fructose corn syrup. It is one of the main reasons I make my own cookies now, because nothing really compares with real butter, sugar and good-quality chocolate. If you're going to have it, make sure it's exceptional.

As you learn to trust yourself with the real goodies, go out to your favourite restaurant where you know the dishes are made from scratch, order something special and see how satisfied you feel with savouring small amounts.

As you learn to pay attention to your body as you eat, you will notice how your stomach begins to expand and feel fuller. It is important to savour every mouthful consciously and slowly so you stop eating when you feel satisfied, rather than uncomfortably full. Any feeling of food in your stomach, or needing to loosen your belt, is an indication that you have eaten too much. There is never a legitimate reason to eat until it hurts. If you eat unconsciously, while distracted, you deprive yourself of the real pleasure of the food. You get the calories without the bliss. Remember, the more you eat without realising, the more food your stomach needs to fill it up, therefore setting yourself up for constant cravings and hunger pangs.

Mindless snacking is not a French habit, neither is 'preventive' eating, when you eat just in case you may get hungry at an inconvenient time. Hunger is the best seasoning, so it is OK to feel the grumbles. In France, I learned to wait for hunger. When I felt sure that I was physically hungry, I ate. There is a difference between being hungry and ravenous. If you wait until you are excessively hungry, inevitably you will overeat. Once you establish a regular eating routine, you will train your body to feel hungry at mealtimes. Even though Josianne would arrive home from work rather late (around 7pm), she would calmly set about preparing dinner for the family without mindlessly snacking, knowing that she would soon sit down to a delicious meal.

Like a typical Frenchwoman, when shopping for food Josianne shunned all foods that were fat-free, sugar-free or stripped of real flavour in any way, preferring to choose smaller quantities of the real thing. She took her role as 'nutritional gatekeeper' for her family seriously. Highly processed, unnatural or synthetic foods from the supermarket were ignored as she enthusiastically sought out fresh, seasonal produce from the local market. A trip to the fresh food market with Josianne was both entertaining and educational. The vendors knew her well as she flirted and fluttered her eyelashes to ensure she got the best cuts of meat, the freshest fish and the tastiest tomatoes. Even though the pursuit of good quality, seasonal produce filled with vitamins and minerals can be more of a challenge in some circumstances (often fresh markets are only open on certain days), the effort is repaid tenfold in the kitchen. It may be a case of having to alter your shopping routine so you can catch the local market, but it is worth it.

Like many of the great chefs repeatedly say, you really can't go wrong when you start with quality. It is also beneficial to eat fat to lose fat, if it's the heart-healthy monounsaturated fat found in olive oil, eggs and avocados, which can actually tame your appetite. This is a key secret of the French paradox. A diet rich in good fats stimulates a feeling of satiety, which promotes an extended sense of satisfaction after eating even small amounts. You may be delighted to learn that brie eaters stay fuller for longer and a small wedge is all you really need.

A plentiful intake of pure, filtered water is the ideal beverage of choice and in my experience always served in French homes with dinner, along with small amounts of red wine of course. The French have a saying, 'A day without wine is like a day without sunshine'—they really savour their wine with dinner, sipping rather than gulping, and certainly never drinking to get rolling drunk. All soft drinks, even diet drinks, are considered detrimental to health and weight. They are not everyday drinks and, even though it may be hard, giving up soft drink is one of the simplest things you can do to take back your health and let go of that weight. Dessert was often fresh seasonal fruit or a small tub of natural yoghurt eaten with half a teaspoon honey or a teaspoon of 100 per cent fruit spread for sweetness. Ice-cream, crepes and cakes were generally eaten outside the home or for special occasions such as birthday parties, dinner parties or at a restaurant.

Cookies, sweets, pastries, potato crisps, salty nuts, pizza and junky chocolate were simply not kept in the house. Thankfully for me. Often the biggest stumbling block is having our cupboards and fridges full of junk food, so that is what we automatically reach for. But Josianne simply didn't shop for junk. She preferred to save indulgences for the ritual of a long Sunday lunch when she would head to the local patisserie early and purchase a selection of mouthwatering, artisanal gateaux for the family to enjoy after the leisurely midday meal.

There was, however, always rich, dark bitter chocolate (containing 70 per cent cocoa mass) in the cupboard, a favourite of Josianne's. I quickly learned that it was almost physically impossible to overindulge in the dark, bitter variety.

By not having access to junk food at home, I was unable to eat automatically and mindlessly whatever temptations were before me. That taught me that the best way to break the habit is not to have stores of your personal trigger foods—the foods that once you start eating, you can't stop—so they lose their power over you. A craving would often subside just with the thought of having to go out to buy it. If I were really desperate for a sugar fix I ate a couple of dried apricots or dates or a piece of fresh fruit and drank a cup of tea (no sugar, of course), which tided me over to the next meal.

As you can probably guess, as a result of my childhood, sugar was definitely my weakness—so sweet, yet so detrimental when consumed to excess. People with a serious sweet tooth suffer from a yo-yo condition of hypoglycaemia (low blood sugar). They crave something sweet to give them energy. Soon after eating it they get a short energy hit, but then come crashing down as insulin kicks in to try to normalise the levels, followed by more sugar cravings to bring the levels back up again. Just like alcohol and cigarettes, sugar is highly addictive and excessive consumption can really sabotage permanent weight loss.

I remember Josianne gasping in horror as I heaped *confiture à la fraise* (strawberry jam) onto my baguette in the morning and piled white sugars into my coffee. The French instinctively know to use sugar very sparingly, so she was naturally alarmed at my heavy hand. I slowly registered that her concern was valid and started to cut back on my sugar intake—I eventually cut it by half.

The French are rather conservative when it comes to sugar, and for good reason. It is already hidden in many everyday foods, even savoury ones. I stopped craving sugar by changing my taste for it, not by cutting out foods such as fresh fruit that naturally contain it. Fortunately, losing your sweet tooth is easy to do—just gradually remove the excess sugar from your life. This can be achieved in steps, each week cutting out more obvious sweetness from your food. I found the weaning approach more appealing than going cold turkey.

In order to cut down on sugar, eliminate those products with additive sugars, such as sweets, cookies, ice-cream and sweetened drinks. These should be occasional foods, rather than everyday staples in your eating routine. Even those who drink caffeine in coffee, tea or cola drinks experience a double rush and a double crash. Ironically, the very substance that picks you up is the one thing that drains you. The interesting fact was that as I broke my addiction to excess sugar, the less I ate, the less I craved. I had simply toned down my sensitivity for the taste of sugar.

Adopting these new French habits did take me some practice, just as changing any old learned behaviour does, but I found that taking small steps every day leads to significant success for the rest of your life. It takes approximately twenty-eight days to change an old habit into a new one, so don't be in a hurry. Give yourself the time to succeed.

Here are my 'golden rules' to get you started on your road to success.

GOLDEN RULES

- Eating should always be a pleasurable experience. Never eat until your tummy hurts! Instead, stop eating when you feel satisfied rather than when you are uncomfortably full.

- When you begin to feel good about your relationship with food, you will naturally discard unsatisfying eating situations and unappealing foods.
- Try cutting your additive sugar consumption by half, by eating less sugar and therefore craving less.
- Thought and effort about what you eat pays off. Shopping for fresh food and preparing a simple meal at home will benefit you in countless ways.
- If you don't shop for them (things like cookies, potato crisps, sweets, junk and processed foods) and keep them at home, you won't eat them mindlessly. When you learn to trust yourself, go ahead and have a quality 'treats' cupboard.
- Learn what a just portion size is (ten fries are better than three hundred) and embrace the concept of quality over quantity.
- Fresh water is all you need to quench your thirst, so drink plenty of it (you can always drink more).
- Red wine is to be savoured with food at mealtimes and in moderation.
- Loving yourself and your body is a useful tool if you want to feel good naked and smile when you look in the mirror.
- Be active at every opportunity—walk everywhere, ride your bike, take the stairs.
- Eat more salads, soups and vegetables.

❖

LA SOUPE

Soups are an ideal way to boost your intake of vegetables on a daily basis. A cup of homemade soup is warming and nourishing, makes a great snack, an excellent starter to a meal and a light meal in itself. The ones I usually make can be made in twenty minutes or less—some in as little as ten minutes.

MUSHROOM SOUP

Prepared in ten minutes, this robust soup is made with sliced fresh mushrooms from the supermarket. This soup is thickened with polenta, which cooks quickly.

1 tbsp unsalted butter
500g (1lb) mushrooms, sliced
1 onion, sliced thinly
2 cloves garlic, crushed
2 litres (3½pt) chicken stock
60g (2oz) instant polenta
2 tbsp heavy cream
salt and pepper to taste

Heat the butter in a large saucepan, then add the mushrooms, onion and garlic and cook over high heat for 3 minutes. Add the stock and bring to the boil. Whisk in the polenta, cover and simmer for about 5 minutes. Add the cream, salt and pepper and serve immediately.

CREAM OF PUMPKIN SOUP

If you have limited time, cut and peeled pumpkin can be found at your greengrocers. With some chicken stock and cream at hand, this soup can be ready in no time.

2 tbsp olive oil
1 onion, diced
2 cloves garlic, sliced
500g (1lb) pumpkin, peeled and cut into small chunks
2 medium potatoes, peeled and quartered
2 litres (3½pt) chicken stock
2 tablespoons heavy cream
salt and pepper to taste

Heat the oil in a large saucepan and sweat the onion and garlic until transparent. Add the chopped pumpkin and potatoes and cook for about 3 minutes. Add the chicken stock, bring to the boil, cover and simmer for 20 minutes. When the vegetables are cooked through, season to taste and add the cream. Using a handheld blender, puree the soup until light and fluffy. Serve immediately.

SPINACH, CANNELLINI BEAN AND PEA SOUP

This soup is another quick and easy meal—filling, nutritious and prepared in a matter of minutes. When making soups, it is always better to make your own stock and use fresh vegetables. But if you are pressed for time, then using frozen vegetables is a fine and convenient option.

Using frozen chopped spinach and baby peas and a can of cannelini beans makes this one a real short-cut soup.

2 tbsp olive oil
1 onion, diced
2 cloves garlic, sliced
500g (1lb) frozen chopped spinach
200g (7oz) frozen baby peas
1 x 400g (14oz) can of cannellini beans, drained
1 litre (1¾pt) chicken stock
salt and pepper to taste

Heat the oil in a large saucepan and add onion and garlic. Cook over high heat until transparent and then add the spinach, peas and cannellini beans. Pour over the chicken stock and bring to the boil. Simmer for about 20 minutes, season to taste and serve.

ONION SOUP
This classic soup can be prepared in very little time. It can be served as a simple lunch, or as part of an evening meal.

20g (½oz) butter
8 onions, evenly sliced
2 heads garlic, peeled and finely chopped
250ml (8fl oz) white wine
2 litres (3½pt) beef stock
1 tbsp thyme

6 diagonal slices stale baguette
50g (1¾oz) gruyere cheese, grated

In a heavy saucepan, heat the butter, add the onions and cook gently until caramelised. Add the garlic, cook for another two minutes and then add the wine, beef stock and thyme. Simmer the liquid for at least 20 minutes. To make the croutons, grill the baguette slices on one side. Turn over, sprinkle with grated gruyere and grill until the cheese is golden and bubbling. Serve the soup immediately with cheesy croutons on top.

4. Eating With Pure Awareness

After one taste of French food ... I was hooked. I'd never eaten like that before, I didn't know such food existed.

—Julia Child

Prior to moving to Paris to live with Frederic's family, my meals were rarely a contemplative experience. I shovelled breakfast down hurriedly with my eyes and ears glued to the morning television program, barely pausing to finish one mouthful before I followed it with another. I often ate lunch in a hurry between clients at work so I could squeeze in time to get to the bank in my lunch break. By the time I made it home again, exhausted, I ate dinner hurriedly while catching snippets of the evening news. The more traumatic the latest news stories were, the more I ate and the less I tasted. Often I would sneak in a well-deserved snack while surfing the web and checking my emails after dinner, and when my hand would inevitably scrape the bottom of the M&M packet, I would curse myself and go to bed in a state of disappointment.

For years I did a lot of swallowing, but not much tasting. The food was present, but my mind wasn't. It never occurred to me that the stomach doesn't have tastebuds. I ate so quickly that often the food flew right past my mouth and slid straight down the oesophagus! When I finally learned to eat mindfully, with pure awareness, I realised that I had cheated my tastebuds unnecessarily for years. When your mind is not concentrating on the experience of eating, it's difficult to keep track — a bit like when you're reading a book and after turning several pages, you realise you can't remember a word of what you have just read. It's the same with eating. If you don't give food your full attention, it is very easy to overeat and to never feel really satisfied.

It sounds so simple, eating while being fully in the moment, but so many of us are in the habit of eating unconsciously, with our thoughts a million miles away. It is so easy to get caught up in your own thoughts that you are scarcely aware of what—and how much—you are eating. Instead you swallow your fears, frustrations, sorrow, your past and your future. You keep eating beyond comfort, out of habit, even to the point of having to loosen your belt, because you are oblivious to what you are doing. Your habits feel familiar and comfortable, even when they're uncomfortable and work against you. The strength of your psychological hunger and the stress of your life cause you to override all your inner satiety signals. When you eat unconsciously and without pure awareness, you only deprive yourself(s) of the total pleasure of the food. You get all the calories, without the bliss.

Being fully aware of the act of eating, both physically and mentally, is just one of the ways that the French manage to feel satisfied with less food. Forget eating while multitasking. The French believe mealtimes should be strictly reserved for food in order to derive the most pleasure from the experience. At the typical family table, the television, telephones and computers are off and the only focus is on the enjoyment of the meal. Eating is designed to be emotionally as well as physically satisfying. If you watch television or surf the web while eating a meal, you will have been distracted from enjoying much of your food. Ultimately, the distraction will leave you unsatisfied and wanting more.

Like many people, you may tend to eat automatically, in somewhat of a trance. Once you get your hand on a fork, there is little chance of stopping the hand to mouth motion until all the food is gone. To counteract this habit, you must remain hyperconscious of your thoughts and actions for a specific period, prior to and during eating, until pure awareness becomes automatic. Try to bring your mind back to your body while you eat. If you are in the habit of eating on autopilot and find it difficult to stop, try getting up from the table to fetch a drink to break the hand-to-mouth spell. If eating feels too good and you struggle to stop, aim to follow eating with something equally as pleasurable.

Slowing down your eating pace begins when you realise that, when it comes to eating, there are no prizes for finishing first. If you plan on having dessert, rest assured it will still be there when you are ready. As a former speed eater (and indigestion sufferer), I found that a brief meditation before meals really helped to centre me emotionally. Simply close your eyes and take a few deep breaths, realise that you are in the presence of food, and start paying attention to your body as you eat. Tune in to your level of hunger—your internal cue—rather than being influenced by the portion size served to you, which is the external cue. Try stopping in the middle of your meal for one or two minutes. Give the food time to hit the bloodstream and then check in with your fullness level. The French meal is typically served in several small courses, so there is automatic pausing between each course.

In the French home, usually large platters and bowls of food are placed at the centre of the table and everyone serves their desired amount, according to their hunger level.

When I first arrived in Paris to work as an au pair, I remember preparing a meal of pasta and salad for the family and automatically dishing up each individual plate. I unknowingly served too much to the children and gave Monsieur too little. Madame politely told me to put it all back and let everyone serve themselves. Even in some French bistros, a communal bowl of chocolate mousse is handed around to each diner. The idea is to listen to your own body and eat according to how hungry you feel on any particular day, rather than have someone else dictate what and how much you should eat. Interestingly, in my experience of looking after French children, I never once encountered a mother who pressured her child to finish everything on their plate.

In order to slow down your eating pace, try sipping between bites. This will give you time between each forkful and keep you from packing one continuous bite on top of the other, which prevents you from savouring the food. You cannot really enjoy the bite in your mouth if there's another waiting on your fork. Do the same thing if you are eating a sandwich. Take your hands off the food while there is a bite in your mouth. Focus on the taste, texture and aroma of each bite as it unravels on your tongue. Try looking up from the food and enjoying the company.

The very essence of the family dinner is to have the opportunity to spend time together. Try taking smaller bites, as this will allow you to savour the food for longer. Rather than devouring the whole piece of pizza, apple or cookie in three large bites, play a game to see how many bites you can get out of your food. While eating with my French family in Paris, I was forced to slow my eating right down in order to keep pace with the rest of the table, and I found I felt a lot better for it. When you feel you are politely full, place the knife and fork on the plate and push the plate away, as a symbolic gesture to signify you are finished eating.

In the event that you are satisfied but are fighting the mental battle of wanting to continue eating, aim to follow eating with something equally as interesting and pleasurable. Maybe plan to leave the table and run a bubble bath, read an absorbing book, go for a stroll or watch your favourite television show. If you are midway through a three-course dinner at your favourite restaurant and no longer feel hungry but are still very much looking forward to the dessert course, you need to get creative and pace yourself. Start dissecting the dish in front of you and only eat the best bits. When the tiramisu arrives, skim your fork through the best bits and savour the smallest amount. Let the creamy mascarpone, coffee and cocoa notes melt on your tongue. You will still be with the company, still enjoying the flavours, but you will not really be consuming much food. Remember, there is never a legitimate reason to eat past satisfaction.

5. The Ten Steps to Losing Weight

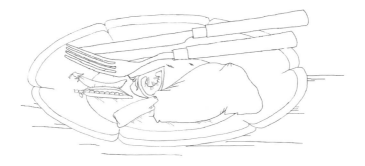

One cannot think well, love well, sleep well, if one has not dined well.
—Virginia Woolf

The real key to permanently changing your dietary habits is to take small steps, so that the results will be lasting. Simply understanding where you have been going wrong is not enough to eliminate the negative eating habits that you've probably had most of your life. These eating patterns have been reinforced by beliefs and actions, and to replace them you need to combine understanding with new behaviour.

For example, if you want to give up soda and sugary drinks, try substituting sparkling water with a touch of lime juice cordial or a squeeze of lemon or orange juice. Gradually, you will not need to add the cordial and you will feel satisfied with a squeeze of fresh lemon. If you are in the habit of visiting the vending machine at four o'clock in the afternoon for a fix to elevate your energy levels, try planning ahead by having a healthy alternative on hand. Order less when you're out and see how satisfied you feel with that amount. If you're used to having several coffees in the morning, try having one freshly brewed, really savouring it, followed by a cup of herbal tea. Try serving your breakfast cereal in a cup rather than a bowl to ensure the correct portion size. If you habitually opt for the drive thru and the inevitable dashboard dining on your way home from work, plan ahead in the morning so that you have something healthy to come home to.

Getting to know your personal triggers is the first step in learning how to manage them effectively. Sometimes wanting to eat when you are not really hungry is just boredom or procrastination. When you are on the prowl for stimulation, or looking for a way to avoid a task, understand that the solution doesn't always have to be in the refrigerator.

Establishing your own replacement habits is a useful way to create a new set of behaviours that will work in your favour. If you know you have a difficult piece of work to get done and you immediately start looking for food to help you through it, try creating a plan for yourself. If you know you are not hungry because you just ate lunch, then you need to have a back-up plan. Perhaps check in with your feelings and identify the trigger (procrastination), then focus on work for thirty minutes, before stopping to have a hot cup of tea. Often this awareness and reassurance is all you need to help you through those difficult times.

When you are sleep-deprived or overtired, you may be on the prowl for food when what you really need is sleep. Sleep is fundamental to good health and weight management. Sleep restores the levels of leptin in the body, an important hormone that gives the brain information about the adequacy of the body's energy stores. When you don't get enough sleep, this hormone doesn't function properly. This is why, after a sleepless night, you may feel that no matter what you eat nothing really satisfies you. When leptin levels go down, usually your appetite goes up, so it is difficult to register hunger and fullness. Ideally you should aim for seven to eight hours a night. Try to make restorative and sound sleep a priority in your life. If you have trouble relaxing before bed, try soaking in a warm bath, avoid television or read a good book.

High stress levels are a common reason why people use food as a coping mechanism. We all have stress in our lives, whether you are a highly paid CEO, a student or a stay-at-home mum. If you continue to lean on food to alleviate stress, perhaps you need to look at the amount of stress in your life, and find ways to reduce or manage it better. The mind exerts a strong and powerful influence upon the body, so if you feel overwhelmed with stress, try altering your mental attitude. Often it is not so much the problem itself, but how you view the problem that makes all the difference. In France, time has a life of its own and everyone moves along at their individual pace. But even on the busiest days, the French make lunch a priority and they give themselves time to eat. Unquestionably, stress is part of life. Living in big cities such as Paris or Sydney can be stressful. But when you learn to separate stress from the eating experience, you are better able to enjoy eating and put the role of food in its proper perspective.

These little changes can add up to big results, and you will not even feel deprived. Remember that you have had a lifetime of eating and coping with food in a certain way, so these changes need patience, focus and perseverance. In general, the French diet less because their habits (as follows) are cultural and have been part of their daily rituals and second nature from birth. When you begin to connect the mind with the body you realise it is not so much our biology that causes weight gain, it is our psychology. While nutrition is certainly important, ultimately it is our minds that govern our behaviour. Therefore, learning to establish clarity of thought, which translates into automatic behaviour, is a great place to start initiating change.

Translating these habits into your own culture and daily routine is not as difficult as you may think. It is just a matter of being more aware of why you eat and how you eat it and replacing negative habits with patterns that work for you.

MAKE TIME TO EAT The French hold food sacred and prioritise it in their daily routines. Rather than just rushing quick meals when a slot of time becomes available, make it a ritual and a priority to eat at regular times each day. Instead of inhaling a burger or sandwich in two minutes flat, take enough time to enjoy and savour the meal. Hurried eating can do more to ruin your digestive system than camembert and charcuterie. Even when you are super busy, try to avoid dining while hunched over a desk, walking down the street or driving a car.

You can still eat mindfully even if you are pressed for time — it's just a matter of being mentally present with your food. If you can't find time to stop the car or find a park bench in order to eat, then try rethinking your priorities. To eat more consciously, make sure to sit down, even if you're just having a handful of nuts — go to the table and sit down to eat. Eating should be emotionally as well as physically satisfying. If you eat while doing other things, you will have been distracted from enjoying what you have consumed. Your body will have all the calories without the emotional satisfaction.

If lunch is the main meal, dinner will naturally be a lighter affair. A typical meal can last anywhere from one hour to several hours in France. But what if you don't have that long to eat your meal? My suggestion is to set the timer and make your meal last for a minimum of twenty minutes. Most workplaces allow at least this amount of time for lunch, so you can spend your time eating consciously. For many of you this will seem like an eternity, but I guarantee you will feel fuller and more satisfied with less food and you'll be less inclined to want to snack an hour later.

If you naturally shovel too much into your mouth at one time and have trouble slowing down, try eating with chopsticks, your non-dominant hand or using smaller cutlery. Slowing down your eating pace allows you to truly savour every mouthful, and pay attention to the taste, texture and aroma of your food.

EAT A VARIETY OF FOODS There are no forbidden foods, only inappropriate quantities that create an imbalance. I like to think of eating a variety of small courses, slowly, as the tapas approach, which is actually a Spanish custom but the concept is the same. Ideally every meal should consist of various components. Rather than eating one gigantic plate of spaghetti bolognaise, try cutting down on the pasta and adding a salad, followed by a small wedge of cheese and a piece of fruit. Eating large amounts of the same food at one sitting can be boring and monotonous, so you keep on eating, searching for satisfaction. The first few bites may taste great, and then the pleasure starts to diminish, but you keep eating because that's all there is. Balancing out a meal is why the typical French meal is not made up of only one part. It consists of a variety of three or four small courses, spread out over time, so it keeps your tastebuds engaged and includes more than one food group. The French revel in following the seasons when it comes to choosing their foods, so that tastebuds are being stimulated throughout the entire year. Variety is the spice of life and, in order to stimulate all of our five senses, we have to regularly vary what we eat from day to day and season to season.

NEVER SKIP MEALS As a general rule, it is best not to go more than five waking hours without food. It's easy to think we're being virtuous by working through lunch or skipping breakfast, but going without a meal, particularly breakfast, will only result in overcompensating later on. If you wait too long to eat, chances are you will overeat. In order to keep the metabolism steady, it is best to eat at regular times each day because your body will adjust to this routine. By keeping a regular eating routine, you will train your body to get hungry at convenient times, which makes eating the right things a habit rather than a battle.

DON'T EAT WHILE DOING OTHER THINGS It is amazing how many people eat while driving, working on the computer, talking on the phone, watching the television or reading the newspaper. Eating while distracted can cause you to overeat because it's difficult to keep track of how much you have consumed. Not only that, eating is supposed to satisfy you emotionally as well as physically, so eating while doing something else will only leave you wanting more food.

Give mealtimes your full and devoted attention—your brain needs to register that you have eaten in order to feel satisfied until the next meal.

KEEP HYDRATED We are always hearing how good it is for us, but no natural resource is as undervalued as water. Nothing hydrates our bodies and quenches our thirst like plain water, so make sure you can access it all through the day. When losing weight, the power of water to fill you up in between meals is invaluable. Often when you think you are hungry, you are actually thirsty—so make your first response to hunger a tall glass of water. If you can give up all sugary sports drinks, energy drinks, cordials, sodas, reconstituted juices, syrupy frappacinos, thickshakes and sweetened ice teas and just drink water in between meals, you will be amazed at the results. Liquid calories are a major contributor to the rising levels of overweight people.

MOVE MORE There are plenty of ways to incorporate more exercise into your day without even having to change your clothes. The French walk much more on average per day than, say, Americans or Australians (who are much more car reliant). Having a car in any European city is a challenge. Consequently, the French rely much less on cars to get around, as their cities and towns are more geared towards getting around on foot. But you can always walk more, wherever you live, just by parking your car farther away from your destination or getting off the train one stop early. Why drive around the parking lot battling for the nearest car spot when you can easily find a park farther away and get some walking in? To encourage more walking, comfortable shoes are important, so take a change of shoes in your bag if you need to. Take the stairs at every opportunity, get a bike and ride it as often as you can, clean the house for twenty minutes a day. Limit television watching and take a walk outside instead.

EAT SMALLER PORTIONS One of the most important secrets of the French diet is their ability to understand appropriate portion sizes for any given food. When they choose heavier foods—such as cheese, charcuterie, foie gras or chocolate mousse—they derive great pleasure and feel satisfied with a very small quantity—and have no guilt about it.

It takes training to eyeball the correct serving size. As a rule, always serve yourself less or order less than you think you want and check in with your satisfaction levels after a small amount. Remember, the most joy is in the first few mouthfuls, after which the pleasure starts to diminish.

Often when you buy packaged food, you assume it is suitable for one, but often it contains two to three servings—but you think you should eat the lot! It's best to buy smaller packages of food. You may save money by buying large, but if it means you unwittingly overeat, it will keep you consuming more and weighing more. And try not to eat straight from a large packet. Instead, take a small plate, serve yourself and sit down to enjoy the eating experience.

Making less seem like more is easily achieved by serving smaller quantities on smaller plates and then slowly savouring every mouthful with mindfulness.

In order to gradually reduce your portion size, always start by serving yourself a bit less than you think you need and plan on having seconds if you feel you have to. Wait a little before you decide whether you need more. Don't feel you must finish every last crumb on your plate, especially when eating out, because often what is served in restaurants is suitable for someone who has put in twelve hours of hard labour — use your intuition and take a mini timeout during the meal to assess your fullness level. When you eat out, sometimes you have to waste food, if you can't take it home — otherwise the food will end up on your own waist. You can always share a meal with a friend or just order a starter.

It may take a week or two to adjust your body's hunger clock and to learn to judge the right portion sizes, but there is no failure in learning what is right for you. Ideally, aim to eat enough to sustain you through to the next meal, but not so much that you feel stuffed and want to fall asleep straight after eating. This is about getting to know your own body and tuning in to your real physical hunger, which may vary according to your activity level on any given day.

Eating the right amount can vary from individual to individual according to age, sex, build and level of activity. Be careful of well-meaning friends and family members who encourage you to eat when you're not hungry because feeding you is a way of expressing their love. Say 'no, thank you' firmly. You have a right to say no. Just as good eating habits are contagious, so are bad ones. A real friend does not pressure you to eat more than you need. A real friend accepts your decline of food with grace and respect.

AVOID MINDLESS SNACKING The French very rarely snack outside mealtimes. It's not that having a snack is wrong if you are genuinely hungry, but if you are on the prowl because you're procrastinating or restless — beware. The problem with snacking on highly addictive processed foods is that once you start, the floodgates can open. These foods are designed to get you hooked. You are less likely to get hooked on apples and pears.

Are you really hungry or do you just have the oral urge to chew or chomp to satisfy a taste hunger? If you eat three balanced, satisfying meals a day and drink plenty of water and herbal teas in between, you shouldn't feel the need to snack. So if you're not really physically hungry, then ask yourself what are you hungry for?

If you know you like to stop mid-morning and mid-afternoon and eat something, keep a little of your meal for later, such as a yoghurt, some nuts or a piece of fruit. In other words, pace yourself. There is no right or wrong way, you have to do what makes you feel best.

FOLLOW THE 90–10 PER CENT RULE The French know how to enjoy life and one of the secrets to weight management is living a life of moderation, balance and variety. Most of the time try to eat nutritionally sound meals based on fresh, quality produce—because it is what you eat repeatedly on a daily basis that makes all the difference. Then 10 per cent of the time, eat whatever your heart desires, even if it is a Big Mac—let your hair down, with the knowledge that allowing yourself one decadent dessert or meal will not suddenly mean you wake up fat.

AVOID ADDITIVE SUGARS The French are very careful when it comes to sugar consumption. Believe it or not we can all adjust our taste for sugar, just by cutting down and eating less—and consequently reducing the constant craving. This really is a reprogramming of your sweet tooth, because the more sugar you eat, the more you crave, and vice versa.

And there's no two ways about it. Excess sugar consumption makes you fat. Not the natural sugar found in fresh fruit, but the fake sweeteners such as 'high fructose corn syrup' in many processed foods. Refined sugar has no nutritional value and does not satisfy hunger. To make matters worse, unused sugar in the body simply turns to fat. Start slowly by cutting out sugar in your tea and coffee and avoid consuming soft drinks, concentrated fruit juices and cordials.

In addition to these steps, affirmations and visualisation can be valuable tools to use as you move towards achieving a healthier weight.

An affirmation is a verbal technique that helps you re-program some of your basic belief systems. When you tell yourself throughout the day, 'I will never be slim, I have no willpower, I have given up on the battle to lose weight and get healthy, I'll never be able to look good in clothes,' you reinforce your belief that you are a person who will continue to fail and continue to make poor food choices.

Affirmations can help you change your beliefs. A statement like 'I am naturally slim, fit and healthy' is an affirmation that can be used to counteract this negative belief. We're constantly talking to ourselves, giving ourselves messages and reinforcing our attitudes. An affirmation is a technique for changing this kind of programming from negative to positive. Keep affirmations short, positive and always in the present tense. If you reinforce your inner reality throughout each day by repeating affirmations, you should notice the beginnings of change within a few weeks. This slight change can be enough to encourage you to continue.

Visualisation is like a visual affirmation. Instead of saying 'I am naturally slim, fit and healthy', you imagine yourself eating healthy foods in appropriate quantities and enjoying them, being active and feeling great in your own body. By repeating this visual image, you slowly counteract the way you have been seeing yourself—heavy, eating too much and feeling uncomfortable in your own body. Visualisation is a pictorial affirmation. It works beautifully for people who are visually oriented. If you learn well by seeing, you can keep a photo of yourself at your ideal weight on the fridge or in your diary to look at several times a day. When you continue seeing yourself as you want to be, your behaviour will begin to change.

6. You Are What You Shop For

How can you expect to govern a country that has two hundred and forty-six kinds of cheese?

—Charles de Gaulle

After six months or so of living under the guidance of my adopted French mother, Frederic and I finally moved to an apartment of our own.

By the time I left Josianne's house, I had shed eight kilos in what I would have to admit was a pleasurable and even indulgent experience, just by eating as a traditional French family do.

Never before had I eaten so well, in a way that not only nourished my body but honoured my tastebuds and left me feeling completely satisfied. I had rediscovered the joy of eating, after years of diet-induced guilt. I also understood the value in making time to shop, prepare and cook good food. There is no better way to feel part of Paris than to engage in the most Parisian of pastimes—shopping at the street markets.

By waiting for true physical hunger, I realised that that's when foods tastes best. By eating mindfully in an inviting environment, I had began to acknowledge and derive great pleasure from the subtle nuances of flavours in my food, which I had previously ignored. When my slender French friend Valerie raved about the salted butter from Normandy she discovered at the market, I shared her excitement, because I now knew the difference. As I learned to listen to my body's innate wisdom, I became aware of how my stomach expanded and began to feel fuller as I ate. With this awareness, I found I was easily able to stop eating at satisfaction.

Remarkably, I never once counted a calorie or fat gram. What I did do was stop snacking mindlessly, drink plenty of water, walk everywhere and eat more fresh fruit, salads, vegetables and yoghurt. I also ate small amounts of cheese, chocolate and bread and drank a little red wine with dinner. The results were somewhat of a miracle, because for once in my life I didn't consider myself to be actually 'on a diet'. I managed to feel satisfied with much smaller quantities than ever before. When I did choose heavier foods, they gave me great pleasure—and I felt no guilt. With regular balanced meals, I lost the insatiable desire to devour large bags of sweets and slurp sugary drinks. As I felt more comfortable in my own body, my self-talk became positive and noncritical. The mystery of the French paradox was beginning to unravel as I embraced my newfound equilibrium.

Moving out to our own apartment was the real test for me because I needed to shop and cook 'French style' and stick to a routine that worked around my busy schedule. I was keen to start implementing all the positive habits I had learned from my mentor Josianne. By this time, I had also started full-time work as a beauty therapist at the luxurious day spa of the Hotel Costes, a fashionable five-star hotel on the right bank of the Seine. Juggling working, having to speak in a foreign language with discerning clients, life in a busy city and keeping house (shopping, cooking, cleaning) meant that suddenly I was doing double duty. On top of this, like most people, I had to find a way to stay healthy because I wanted to maintain my new-found equilibrium, my new appearance and keep up the positive results I had achieved.

Just as Josianne had shown me, the answer lay in carefully planning my time and thinking ahead so that I always had the necessary ingredients to make a balanced meal. I established a routine that made eating the right things a habit rather than a battle and I made sure to keep daily rituals around mealtimes. It was a priority to shop for fresh, nutritious food so that we had nourishing food every day of the week. I also made a point of incorporating incidental exercise into my day at every opportunity. Although challenging, I managed to fit all these needs in and around my busy workload and other responsibilities. The benefits were well worth the extra effort it took.

Usually the best of intentions about how and what you eat, come unstuck when you are extremely busy. Many people are convinced that they have a weight problem because they have a 'time problem'.

But the real dilemma is where your priorities are. People who are 'time poor' often eat on the run or grab take-out, instead of finding and taking the time to eat well. Once you accept that you are worthy of taking the effort to prepare food ahead of time so there is something healthy to eat when you come home after a busy day, you are more likely to make time for a lunch break on even the busiest days. You are more likely to take care of yourself in other ways too—by finding time to be active, practise relaxation and to do something you enjoy, rather than spend all your time working.

The French working week averages thirty-five hours, which makes it conducive to achieving a good work–life balance. It is not selfish to take care of yourself—it's one of the most important things you can do for yourself and your family. If you owned a million-dollar racehorse, how would you feed it? Would you make sure it gets adequate exercise and proper nutrition? Would you make sure it gets just the right amount of food to perform at its peak? Would you make sure it didn't get too stressed so that it remained happy? You can do the same for yourself.

I felt I had learned enough basics from my experience of living with Josianne to be able to cook simple meals. If you have good ingredients on hand, preparing a balanced meal is really not so daunting. Simply grilling fish, chicken, lamb or veal with a little butter, herbs and lemon juice and sautéing some zucchini, mushrooms and red peppers seasoned with olive oil, salt and pepper takes only minutes. But what could be easier and more enjoyable than eating that, followed by a simple green salad, a small, aromatic wedge of camembert and a ripe piece of fruit, savoured with a little red wine? And fortunately, Josianne was never more than a phone call away if I needed advice on the best way to prepare and serve anything. If you don't have someone to call for cooking advice, I highly recommend going online if you can, as the web offers an abundance of ideas.

I am the first to humbly admit that I am no masterchef or cooking school graduate. I have no revolutionary recipes, sophisticated kitchen gadgets or fancy skills in the kitchen — only memorable meals and shrewd observations of my time spent living and dining with the French. But I strongly believe that the key to good health and weight management begins in your own kitchen. You can enjoy wonderful food and still be healthy. All you really need is a willingness to learn the basics.

Think about what you love to eat and then start slowly. If your mother never taught you to cook, it is not too late to start teaching yourself. Choose a repertoire of perhaps ten dishes and work towards perfecting them, so you can wow your family and friends (as well as yourself). It won't take long before you can prepare certain dishes almost with your eyes closed.

The key is being organised and planning ahead so that you have all the ingredients you need to make cooking enjoyable rather than stressful. When you try a recipe for the first time, be sure to read the whole thing through first so you know what you're in for. You may want to make a list and a menu plan before you go shopping. Eventually, with practice, you will learn to shop by instinct.

The French take shopping for food very seriously. It is probably as important and sacred as eating the food. The quality of your ingredients is paramount. The food needs to look 'alive'. Without fresh, seasonal and quality ingredients, your cooking will be no good, so make it your quest to buy great produce. Frequent your local market once or twice a week and stock up on a variety of brightly coloured fruits and vegetables—whatever looks and smells best and is in season. With shopping, many people settle into a rut about what they cook—and the types of vegetables and fruit they buy.

Depending on the time of year, let your nose and eyes guide you and inspire you to try new things that you may have never tried before or do not usually consider. And don't be afraid to add a little butter or olive oil to season your vegetables—if they taste great, you will want to eat them regularly. I still find it difficult to get excited about an undressed salad.

In springtime, look for asparagus, cucumbers, radishes, beetroot, strawberries and kiwis. As a starter, the French will often serve sliced cucumbers, coated simply in a sauce of olive oil, lemon juice and a dash of cream and seasoned with salt and pepper. Radishes are cut and served with a little butter and salt. Asparagus gets thrown into an omelette, made into soup or sliced up, mixed with white sauce and baked in puff pastry. Beetroot is peeled, grated and tossed in vinaigrette to make a salad. Succulent ripe strawberries are often served with a little sweetened whipped cream.

In summertime, revel in ripe tomatoes, snow peas, avocados, rocket (arugula) leaves, peppers, zucchini (courgettes), nectarines, peaches, mangoes, berries and watermelon. The warmest months are the ideal time for salads, stone fruits and chilled rose. Ruby red tomatoes are sliced and tossed in vinaigrette dressing as a salad. Or they get sliced, gutted and stuffed with prawns coated in mayonnaise, tossed into an omelette or made into a savoury tart. With red capsicums and zucchini at their peak, I enjoy stuffing them with a little mince, herbs, parmesan and breadcrumbs and baking them until bubbly and golden. Berries are made into soufflés, syrups and mousses. Peaches get poached in white wine or champagne or serve 'melba style' with redcurrant jelly and crème anglaise. Watermelon is simply enjoyed on its own.

In the autumn months, enjoy wild mushrooms, fennel, spinach, eggplant (aubergines), mandarins, golden delicious apples, pears and figs. I can't recall eating eggplant growing up, but now it is one of my favourite vegetables. Simply grilled with olive oil or made into a dip, a ratatouille or a gratin, eggplant is surprisingly versatile. Fennel bulbs are sliced and served on their own in bars with aperitifs, but are even better sliced and sautéed with butter as a side dish. Mushrooms can be thrown into casseroles, especially my favourite, *boeuf bourguignon*. They can be grilled with herbed butter, made into soups, folded into omelettes and sautéed with cream and escalopes of veal. Pears are poached in wine or made into sumptuous tarts. Sweet apples are perfect in tarts too and get stuffed and baked, flambéed and pureed.

Winter is the time to buy leeks, potatoes, broccoli, cauliflower, carrots, juicy navel oranges, grapefruits and pears. In the colder months, I enjoy making a vichyssoise, otherwise known as potato and leek soup—it can be served hot or at room temperature. Carrots can be sliced, fried with a little bacon and left to simmer in chicken stock until tender or used with celery to flavour casseroles. Broccoli and cauliflower are wonderful baked in the oven in a cheese sauce or steamed and served with shavings of parmesan cheese. Ripe navel oranges are delicious too, peeled, sliced and left to marinate in a little castor sugar and rum. Potatoes are endlessly versatile and are made into frites, mashed, sautéed, steamed and served au gratin.

Of course many fruits and vegetables are readily available all year round now, but they taste better in their true season. We really are spoiled for choice when we go market shopping, but always try to buy local produce that's in season.

I believe in cooking light wherever possible, but there are some cases where it just doesn't work. For instance, the French just don't use non-fat or even low-fat mayonnaise or cream. Such products can compromise the integrity of a dish. Fatty ingredients like butter, cream and mayonnaise carry flavour throughout a dish—and without flavour they are nothing. Eating full-fat ingredients in appropriate quantities will not result in weight gain. The wonderful thing is it only takes a tiny amount to do the job. But you can't eat sticks of butter every day and expect to lose weight. It's all a matter of balance.

Changing the way you shop for food will definitely change the perimeter of your waistline. Junky food results in chunky bodies. Shopping is as much about what you don't buy as it is about what you do buy, so aim to purchase only real whole foods rather than overly processed foods. A good general rule is if you think your great-grandmother wouldn't recognise it, don't buy it! Much of what is being sold these days cannot really be considered 'real food'. It is packaged, preserved, often laden with colours and chemicals, made to look exciting and sold as something that is 'good for you'.

The less human interference a food has had, the better it is for you. Natural, whole foods are best. Why eat an apple flavoured fruit stick when you can just eat an apple? Why drink the reconstituted juice, when you can eat the piece of fruit instead? Valuable fibre in the fruit will keep you fuller for longer. Why eat a banana-flavoured fruit bar when you can eat a banana instead?

It may not be rocket science, but if you eat more vegetables and fruit, lean protein, fish, pulses and whole grains and less burgers, fries, pizza and doughnuts you will lose weight. It's not that you shouldn't treat yourself once in a while, but what you eat the most of on a daily basis is what counts in the long run. If you don't shop for junk and don't keep it at home, you won't be tempted to live on it.

Try your best to shop at a fresh food market, but if you only have convenient access to a supermarket, stick to the perimeter of the store where most of the fresh produce is. Take a list with you, so you can remember what you intended to buy in the first place and try not to shop on an empty stomach, when you feel ravenous and easily tempted to impulse buy.

In the initial stages of changing your old habits, I suggest you don't even walk down the aisles of temptation! Learn to put your blinkers on when you go shopping. If you decide in advance what you want to buy, you will be more likely to follow through with your plan. Why look at all the cookies, confectionary, chips and soft drinks when you don't need them?

There are certain non-perishable pantry and refrigerator items you can keep on hand. When you make simple vinaigrette, keep the leftover dressing in a screw-top jar ready to shake and use at your convenience. You don't have to use a bottled dressing from the supermarket (it's full of preservatives). Other things to keep in your refrigerator are anchovies, capers, a good quality Dijon mustard and whole egg mayonnaise, Tabasco sauce and ketchup. Some items need to be bought regularly as they are semi-perishable: chunks of parmesan (preferably parmigiano-reggiano), black and green olives, eggs, butter, small amounts of full-fat cream, a variety of cheeses (brie, feta, gruyere), lemons and fresh herbs such as basil, parsley, chives, thyme and rosemary. If you can grow some herbs in your garden or on your window sill, it's even better.

Over a period of a month or two, you can gradually stock your pantry with essentials. Start with best quality sea salt and peppercorns for grinding. Assorted dried herbs (thyme, tarragon, Provençal herbs, bay leaves and oregano) and spices (cinnamon, cumin, nutmeg, cayenne pepper, curry powder, paprika and ginger). Buy a good extra virgin olive oil, red and white wine vinegars, balsamic vinegar and canola oil. Keep some red and white wine for cooking and some organic stock cubes, or good-quality stock in cartons (vegetable, chicken, beef and fish). Stock up on canned tuna, red salmon, beans such as cannellini, bortalotti and chickpeas. Jars of artichoke hearts, roasted red peppers and semi-dried tomatoes are good for impromptu meals and tomato paste and chopped Italian tomatoes in cans are essential for casseroles and sauces.

Here are some of my favourite dishes, the ones that I like to make regularly. My friends and family say they love them and yet they are all so easy to make. I am a one-pot woman in my kitchen because I hate cleaning up — or, in fact, creating a big mess and therefore giving myself too much work to do.

SALMON PARCELS WITH LEMON AND ROSEMARY

This is a fresh, light main course which is wonderfully quick and easy to prepare. It is great to eat in summer with a leafy green salad or served with steamed jasmine rice or new potatoes.

4 skinless salmon filets
2 cloves garlic, crushed
1 small sprig rosemary, finely chopped
1 tbsp olive oil
a squeeze of lemon juice
salt and pepper to taste

Preheat the oven to 180°C (350°F). Place each salmon fillet in the centre of a small sheet of foil and season well with salt and pepper. In a separate bowl, whisk together the crushed garlic, the chopped rosemary, olive oil and the lemon juice and then pour the marinade over the fish. Gently fold over the foil pieces to form parcels and place the parcels on a baking tray. Put the tray into the heated oven for about 10–12 minutes. Remove the parcels and serve immediately. SERVES 4

SAUTEED FISH WITH TAPENADE AND BUTTERED CABBAGE

100g (3½oz) stoned black olives
1 tsp capers, drained
2 anchovy fillets
1 clove garlic
1 tbsp olive oil, plus extra for frying
1 tbsp butter, plus 1 tsp
¼ cabbage, shredded
¼ tsp nutmeg
250g (8oz) white fish fillets
salt and pepper to taste

Place the olives, capers, anchovy fillets and garlic in a blender and blitz until smooth, then add the olive oil. Decant into a small clean screw-top jar. Alternatively, you can buy a jar of black olive tapenade. Heat 1 tablespoon of butter in a pan and add the shredded cabbage; sauté until softened and slightly coloured, then season with salt, pepper and nutmeg. In another pan, heat a little olive oil and a teaspoon of butter and sauté the fish fillets for about 2 minutes on each side. Serve the fish on a bed of cabbage with a generous spoonful of tapenade. SERVES 2

CREAMY VEAL WITH MUSHROOMS

This is delicious served with couscous and buttered green beans. Buy the white veal, which has a velvety texture.

500g (1lb) white veal, in thin strips
¼ cup plain flour
1 tsp smoky paprika
1 tsp butter
1 tbsp olive oil
2 cups sliced mushrooms
2 tbsp cream
parsley, finely chopped
salt and pepper to taste

Mix together the flour, paprika, salt and pepper. Coat the veal strips in the flour mixture thoroughly. Heat the butter and olive oil in a large pan. When the butter starts to froth, toss in the veal and sauté until browned. Add the sliced mushrooms and cook a further 5 minutes. Turn off the heat and add the cream to the pan. Garnish with parsley. SERVES 4

LAMB CUTLETS AND HERBED LENTILS

1 tbsp olive oil
1 onion, diced
1 x 400g (14oz) can brown lentils, drained and rinsed
a handful of mint leaves, chopped
1 tbsp red wine vinegar

100g (3½oz) feta cheese, crumbled
6 lamb cutlets

Heat the olive oil in a pan, add the onion and cook until soft.
Add the lentils, mint and vinegar and heat through. Take off
the heat and mix through the feta. Grill the lamb cutlets to
your liking and serve on top of the lentils. SERVES 2

BRAISED CHICKEN WITH ARTICHOKES, OLIVES AND BABY PEAS

This is easy to throw together and requires no effort as you
wait for it to cook, so you can relax in the interim.

2 tbsp olive oil
1 red onion, diced
4 cloves garlic, sliced
1kg (2¼lb) chicken thigh fillets, diced
1 x 400g (14oz) can diced tomatoes
400g (14oz) frozen baby peas
200g (7oz) marinated artichoke hearts
100ml (3½fl oz) white wine
1 bay leaf
100g (3½oz) marinated split green olives (available at the deli)
salt and pepper to taste

Heat the oil in a large pan or casserole dish with a lid and
fry the onion and garlic until softened. Add the chicken and
sauté until brown, then add the tomatoes, peas, artichokes,

white wine, salt, pepper and bay leaf. Cover and simmer for 30–40 minutes, until the chicken is tender, Five minutes before serving, add the split green olives. Serve with sautéed mushrooms and crusty bread. SERVES 6

HERBED CHICKEN TENDERLOINS
AND WHITE BEAN PUREE

Chicken tenderloins are widely available, are almost fat-free and they cook in minutes. The trick is to avoid overcooking them. The best cooking method is to sauté the tenderloins until they are just about done, then leave them to finish cooking in their own heat. This meal can be served with a leafy green salad, dressed blanched green beans or asparagus.

3 tbsp butter, plus a little extra
500g (1lb) chicken tenderloins
2 tbsp herbes de Provence (a blend of dried herbs, usually thyme, sage, fennel, basil and rosemary)
1 onion, diced
1 clove garlic, finely chopped
1 x 400g (14oz) can cannellini beans
juice of 1 lemon
salt and pepper to taste

Melt two tablespoons of butter in a large saucepan, Sprinkle the chicken with herbs, salt and pepper. Place in the foaming butter and cook on each side for about 2 minutes. Cover the pan and set aside off the heat for 8 minutes.

Meanwhile, heat one tablespoon of butter in a separate pan and sweat the onion and garlic, then add the drained and rinsed beans and heat through. Transfer the mixture to a blender and blend until smooth, then add a knob of butter, salt and pepper. To serve, place the chicken tenderloins on a bed of bean puree and squeeze over some lemon juice. SERVES 4

7. Au Revoir to Emotional Eating

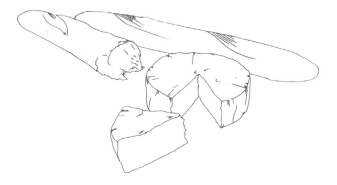

He who distinguishes the true savour of his food can never be a glutton—he who does not cannot be otherwise.

—Henry David Thoreau

When you learn to put food into its proper perspective, you can become more aware of the dozens of ways you may be using it as a means of coping with life. If you turn to food in times of stress or as a way to tolerate the intolerable, you may feel soothed. But using food to cope with difficult emotions, instead of facing them, is only a temporary measure. Eating as a coping mechanism doesn't help you address the underlying thoughts and feelings that make you turn to food in the first place. As difficult as it may be for you to communicate your feelings or even to identify them, it is important to learn to express them with words rather than through eating.

To my French friends, the concept of eating to suppress uncomfortable feelings is more or less a foreign one. They are more adept at finding ways to comfort, nurture, distract and resolve their issues without using food. Food cannot replace feelings and they seem to instinctively understand that no amount of eating is going to fix a problem.

Admittedly, for me eating had always been closely linked with my emotions rather than to true physical hunger. In my family, like many others, we said 'I love you' with food, not words. Eating may give you a warm, comforting satisfaction that's so close to how you feel when you feel loved that you get the two confused. So you may eat when you actually want to feel close to someone and there is no-one to fill this emptiness.

I used to believe eating would miraculously change the way I felt. But the comfort it provided was only fleeting. Food doesn't help you to get to the root of whatever's eating you. When you develop the ability to regulate your own emotions, you can begin to separate using food as a way to cope from using it to nourish your body. If you have trouble expressing your true feelings or perhaps are unaware of how to identify them, you may use food as a crutch, but the eating will not bring you the enjoyment that it should because it will be tainted with regret. I believe emotional eating—specifically eating to change the way you feel or as a coping mechanism—is a big culprit for the rising rate of obesity in the world today.

In order to lose weight and keep it off, it is important to develop strategies of mindfully checking in with your emotions, so you can pay careful attention to what your body needs and wants at any given moment. Whether it is writing your feelings in a journal, having some contemplative time or self-talk, connecting with your emotions is the key to understanding them better. You can learn to connect with yourself. Doing this also requires learning what to do when the thing that your body and mind needs and wants is not food. A ten-minute walk outside, a telephone call to an understanding friend or a soak in the bathtub can help you to feel nourished without the use of food. Rather than eat to resolve emotional issues, my motto, when faced with an emotional food craving, is to talk it out, walk it out or take steps to sort it out. Never use food to cope with a crisis or as a solution to your problems.

Many people know about the importance of healthy eating and exercise, but it is crucial to master the emotions needed for successful weight loss. If permanent weight management were as simple as following a calorie-controlled meal plan, then no-one would have a weight problem. Believe it or not, weight is not the real problem. Excess weight is the symptom of the problem, so it is important to get to the root cause of what is causing you to make poor food choices and to overeat. You may need to look at the amount of stress in your life and make adjustments to your lifestyle.

People misuse food for many different reasons, but emotional eating is probably one of the main hurdles you need to face in order to lose weight and keep it off. Awareness and understanding are the first steps you need to take. But the real solution is action. Action requires finding positive replacement habits that you can learn to do without a second thought. If you've had a hard day at work and your first instinct is to reach for the chocolate cake, try calling a friend to talk. Perhaps take a walk in the fresh air to clear your thoughts or soak in a warm bath before dinner.

An emotionally cued eater often eats without being fully in the present. Or they eat outside of their own awareness when their thoughts are a million miles away. Typically, they swallow but they don't really taste their food. In fact, when people eat emotionally for reasons other than physical hunger, rather than feel uplifted, they often feel worse afterwards once the feelings of guilt and regret set in.

In order to overcome emotional eating you need focus, calmness, determination, resilience, optimism and emotional energy. There is no failure—because every emotional trigger to overeat is an opportunity to learn more about yourself. After all, you need to get to the root of what is causing you to overeat emotionally and then find ways to manage your personal triggers.

It may be the stress of unresolved issues, relationship problems, work stress, financial worries or even the winter blues. More and more evidence shows that stress is just as harmful to your weight as it is to your heart. By knowing what triggers you to overeat emotionally, you can be prepared to manage the situation before it arises, rather than let it be detrimental to your wellbeing. Stress-related and emotional eating often leads not only to overconsumption but to poor digestion. If you can resolve what causes the overeating, you will stop overeating and lose the excess weight. Try some deep breathing or meditation to help you through the moments you feel the compulsion to eat when you are not physically hungry.

The French perceive themselves to be a slim nation (there is almost a cultural aversion to obesity), which is one of the fundamental characteristics of their mindset and a big reason why they have a lower than average obesity rate. Based on my experience, it is apparent that because of their structured eating routine, choosing healthy things to eat is a habit rather than a battle. The tradition of eating mindfully means they are able to eat less but enjoy it more. Scoffing down food and drink while driving the car, walking or travelling on the metro is the exception rather than the rule.

My French friends don't turn to food when they're upset, because food doesn't have the power to overwhelm them. Rather than use food to replace feelings, the French are more likely to talk, often with family and friends. They also love a good debate, so verbalising their opinions and

emotions comes naturally. When you learn to express yourself and enjoy yourself without food, it no longer needs to
be a substitute. Food in France is kept in its proper perspective—as a way to nourish the body, sustain a vibrant life and
as pleasure for the senses.

If you sense that you are an emotionally cued eater, and
that it is keeping you from reaching a healthy weight, try
asking yourself honestly: why are you overfeeding yourself?
Is it because you want to:

hide from shame
drown loss
forget the memory
escape from trauma
ignore a bad relationship
avoid disappointment
shortcut grief
suppress dashed expectations?

Gradually you will become adept at separating biological
hunger signals from emotional hunger. You may begin to
feel your feelings instead of eat them, so you may experience
discomfort or even sadness. But you will become better at
finding ways to comfort and distract yourself without the
use of food. There is one big difference between people who
are successful at losing weight and keeping it off compared
with those who are not good at it. If you continue to eat
based on emotional hunger, your body will never feel satis-

fied by food but you will continue to blame the food. This is why many people think that they never feel full—they never get the signal to stop eating because they were using food for emotional fulfilment.

The good news is that you can easily learn to distinguish between genuine hunger and emotional hunger—just by stopping and asking yourself 'Am I physically hungry or do I just want to change the way I feel?'

If you feel you have some unresolved issues relating to your past, no amount of food will make it go away. In this case, it is worth seeking professional help.

In many cases the urge to eat is actually more of a need to drink, so make your first response to hunger a tall glass of water or a cup of tea. Often that is all you need to carry on until the next meal. If you are genuinely hungry, but a meal is scheduled in an hour's time, pace yourself by eating a small snack such as a small tub of yoghurt, a piece of fruit or a handful of raw nuts, with the view to fully enjoying the meal to come.

The French, like everyone, have their fair share of stresses and emotional issues, but they are more committed to living a relaxed lifestyle. Two-hour lunches, 35-hour working weeks and five weeks annual vacation means that they pace themselves and aim to enjoy life more. They understand that the *petits plaisirs* (little pleasures) we offer ourselves on a regular basis are what makes up a beautiful life. This attitude means that they are not owned by their job, run by their schedule or constantly pressured to overachieve. While working in Paris alongside the French, I found they had a unique ability to shrug their shoulders and let things slide away, like water off a duck's back, rather than get overly stressed and reach for the nearest box of cookies. Josianne also had her fair share of problems, and I would often listen to her talk for hours as she vented them, but she would never turn to a plate of pastries and try to eat her problems away. Try reaching out and talking to a friend or even writing down your problems to better understand what's bothering you. Arriving at awareness and understanding of what's bothering you is more productive than suppressing them with extra food that your body doesn't need.

When you think that no-one else can possibly understand what you've been through and how you feel, when you feel stuck, when you need someone who will take the time to talk with you, turn to people who specialise in working with the same problem. As you reach outside yourself for additional help, you can begin to move forward with your life. The way out of any problem is always through it, there's no way around it. As Winston Churchill once said, 'If you are going through hell, keep going.'

8. Superfoods for Weight Loss

We are indeed much more than what we eat, but what we eat can nevertheless help us to be much more than who we are.

– Adelle Davis

Before I went to live in France, there were certain foods I had never eaten, but grew to love, especially knowing how good they were for weight management and good health. Like many people, I had read countless conflicting articles about what is and isn't good for you, what one should and shouldn't eat. But that led to nothing but confusion about exactly what I should be eating.

After years of dieting, I wasn't sure if I should make an omelette with the yolks or just the whites, whether I should use real butter on my toast or skip it altogether, whether I should eat no-fat cheese or the fabulous full-fat variety. The French approach to eating is ultimately to bring pleasure to the tastebuds, at the same time as nourishing the body, so you should aim to eat whatever pleases and satisfies you the most. The French believe that there are no forbidden foods if you can control the portions. When it comes to eating well as close to natural is always best, even if it does contain fat (as do avocados, egg yolks and nuts, for example).

I learned that there are certain foods that can help you slim down—they rev up your calorie-burning ability and curbing your cravings by providing a greater feeling of satiety. It is no secret that vegetables and fruit are all-natural sources of vitamins, minerals and antioxidants, plus they are filling, so eating plenty of them, along with good-quality protein, on a daily basis should be your goal. Eating complex carbohydrates, such as wholegrain breads, pastas, beans and lentils, which release slowly into the bloodstream will keep you sustained for longer. Ideally, small amounts of simple carbohydrates (sweets) should be eaten following real food, so that the fast release of sugars into the bloodstream has less impact on your moods and your weight.

I never like to be subjected to a 'forbidden food' list, because real food is not the enemy. There are no 'bad' foods, to my mind—it is incorrect portions of certain foods that are the real problem. Some foods work for you, others work against you. Too many junky foods will not help you live a vibrant life, because ultimately they zap your energy. By keeping portion sizes small, you no longer need to view foods as good or bad. I am only really interested in foods that will honour my tastebuds and be of benefit to my overall health. Most weight-loss programs give you a long list of foods that you should avoid like the plague, but the secret of the French diet is that nothing is forbidden. The aim is balance, moderation and variety. We all crave variety in food. Even a week of lasagne will leave you wanting chicken. Paradoxically, because you know that you can have more food of your choosing whenever you are hungry, it's easy to stop eating when you are comfortably full. You naturally let go of the last supper mentality.

Here is a list of some 'super foods'. They benefit not only your health but are sure to help you towards managing a stable weight. Add them to your plate and you will be healthier, slimmer and have more energy for embracing life.

EGGS
Dig in to eggs, yolks and all, they won't harm your heart and can help you trim inches. In the past we were urged to consume no more than three to four eggs per week (because of the cholesterol in the yolk of the egg), now it appears that

eggs do not have as much impact on blood cholesterol as was feared. Egg protein is filling, so you feel fuller for longer. The French often make a meal out of eggs, and a simple omelette flavoured with herbs and accompanied by a green salad is a staple offering in French bistros. At my local café in Paris, hardboiled eggs, still in their shell, were always on offer to accompany the morning coffee.

EAT MORE Omelettes, scrambles and crustless quiches, or simply hardboiled or soft boiled eggs enjoyed with a little salt and pepper. Try this:

ZUCCHINI, FETA AND OLIVE SLICE

1 large onion, diced
3 rashers bacon, lightly fried
5 eggs
100g (3½oz) feta cheese, crumbled
60g (2oz) olive oil
50g (1¾oz) split green olives
¼ cup plain flour
300g (10oz) zucchini (courgettes), grated
salt and pepper to taste

Heat a little olive oil in a frying pan. Fry the onion and bacon in a frying pan and set aside. In a bowl, whisk the eggs, cheese, flour, olive oil, olives together, then add the sautéed onion, bacon and grated zucchini.

Bake in a buttered baking tray in a moderate oven for 30–40 minutes, until golden brown. Serve with leafy green salad.

APPLE CIDER VINEGAR

As well as eating apples regularly, Josianne introduced me to a French secret that I have been using ever since. Every morning, upon rising, she would take a shot of apple cider vinegar, along with a tall glass of water. As well as being an excellent liver cleanser, organic apple cider vinegar is a natural, safe and, some argue, a miraculous elixir.

Apple cider vinegar has been used since ancient times for weight loss and to remedy other ailments. It is thought to help break down fat in your body and dispel waste, thereby helping you lose weight. Apple cider vinegar — in particular the organic, unfiltered variety — is very rich in nutrients, vitamins and minerals.

For weight maintenance, the vinegar is also very helpful because it can speed up your metabolism: reduce your appetite and aid digestion. When consumed in conjunction with a healthy fibre-filled diet, the vinegar can help improve elimination.

For weight loss, it is recommended you take two teaspoons of vinegar mixed in water before every meal. As a maintenance program, just drink a diluted shot upon rising.

EAT MORE You can substitute apple cider vinegar for red or white wine vinegar when you make a simple vinaigrette. It is also a nourishing drink mixed with honey and hot water.

SPINACH

The French consume a lot of spinach and it is as enjoyable in summer as a salad as it is in winter, sautéed with butter and garlic. Spinach is loaded with calcium, folic acid, vitamin K and iron. It is rich in vitamin C, fibre and carotinoids. Add its lutein and bioflavonoids and spinach is a nutritional powerhouse. Fresh or frozen, add this valuable green to your food menu as often as you can.

EAT MORE Add chopped spinach to your favourite vegetable soup or pasta sauce. Add it to omelettes or frittatas — I love to make a spinach and feta cheese omelette as a quick meal. You can sauté spinach with a touch of butter and garlic for a tasty accompaniment to any meal or try a salad made with baby spinach leaves, shavings of parmesan cheese and thin slices of pear. Try these for a light lunch, with a simple salad:

SPINACH TRIANGLES

125g (4oz) frozen spinach, defrosted
1 egg, lightly beaten
½ cup freshly grated parmesan cheese
1 sheet puff pastry
salt and pepper to taste

Preheat the oven to 180°C (350°C). Squeeze the excess liquid out of the spinach. In a bowl, mix together the spinach, egg, cheese, salt and pepper. Cut the sheet of puff pastry into four equal squares. Place a tablespoon of the spinach mixture on the centre of each square and fold over to form a triangle. Press the edges down with a fork, place on a buttered baking tray and brush with milk. Bake until golden brown, around 20 minutes.

OATS

Oat is a cereal that is generally considered to be very soothing for the nerves and good for all-round health. Oats are good for weight loss when eaten in appropriate quantities, beneficial for lowering cholesterol, managing diabetes and reducing toxins in the liver. Having oats regularly can cure constipation, as they have a higher level of soluble fibre than any other grains. All oats are healthy, but the steel-cut or traditional rolled oats (which are minimally processed) contain the most fibre, making them the most filling.

EAT MORE A bowl of warm oatmeal (porridge) in the morning is an excellent breakfast, perhaps along with some fruit and yoghurt that will sustain you until lunch. You can also make burcher muesli, a delicious blend of soaked rolled oats, natural yoghurt, grated apple, honey and cinnamon; you could add fresh berries. It is surprisingly easy to make — try it for breakfast.

APPLE AND CINNAMON BIRCHER

In a bowl, combine one cup rolled oats with ½ cup apple juice and allow it to soak for 10 minutes. Add 1 grated, unpeeled green apple, a pinch of ground cinnamon, a table-spoon of honey and ½ cup of natural yoghurt. Add ¼ cup toasted slivered almonds and mix well. Serve with some fresh berries, if desired.

YOGHURT

The French are one of the highest consumers per capita of yoghurt and it is one of the core secrets of their diet. It is really like a secret weapon—satisfying, nutritious and easy to digest.

Dieticians often refer to plain yoghurt as the perfect food, and for good reason. With its trifecta of carbohydrates, protein and fat, it can stave off cravings for processed foods by keeping blood sugar levels steady. Yoghurt is a wonderful and versatile calcium source, in addition to containing live bacteria, vital to your digestive wellbeing.

All yoghurts are not created equal, so be careful not to choose highly processed yoghurt with 'fruit on the bottom'. There really isn't any fruit on the bottom but, rather, highly sweetened preserves! Plain, unflavoured natural yoghurt is best and if you desire a little sweetness, you can be the one in control of the amount and type of sweetener you add.

EAT MORE Yoghurt as a satisfying snack or dessert. Try adding a teaspoon of honey and a tablespoon of slivered almonds to plain yoghurt, or simply add fresh berries or stewed apples with a little cinnamon.

LENTILS

The French eat a lot of lentils, especially the quick cooking and versatile Puy lentils. They make a great accompaniment to fish, meat and poultry and are a bona fide belly flattener. They are high in protein and soluble fibre and they create a feeling of satiety. Compared with other types of dried legumes, lentils are relatively quick and easy to prepare. They readily absorb a variety of wonderful flavours from other foods and seasonings, so they really are a blank canvas. They can be added to soups and casseroles to help increase fibre in your diet. Not only that, they are available all year round. This tiny nutritional giant fills you up—not out.

EAT MORE Lentil soups, add red or yellow lentils (they cook the fastest) to a pasta sauce for a heartier dish or try a bed of spicy Puy lentils topped with lamb cutlets or a crispy salmon fillet.

FISH

The French love their seafood. I fell in love with mussels and the famous fish soup from Provence, bouillabaisse. You can bake all varieties of fish and seafood whole in the oven, grill it or pan-fry it. Not only do fish fats keep your heart healthy but they help to shrink your waist too. The omega-3 fatty acids they contain improve insulin sensitivity, which helps build muscle and decrease belly fat. We can all benefit from eating more fish and less red meat. Being an excellent protein source with fewer calories, it is often better than other meat sources. Healthy ways to enjoy fish include baked, poached, grilled and steamed.

EAT MORE You don't need to do much to enhance the taste of fish. Season a fillet with salt and pepper and cook in a pan with a tablespoon of oil for a couple of minutes each side and finish with a squeeze of lemon juice.

PARMESAN

Although parmesan cheese is associated with Italian cuisine rather than French, it is widely used and loved by the French. Parmesan is packed full of flavour and a little bit goes a long way. It contains all the goodness of milk but in a concentrated form. So drop that rubbery low-fat cheese and pick up the real stuff.

Due to its long ageing, much of the protein in parmesan has been broken down—in effect, the protein has been 'pre-digested' and as a result puts very little strain on the metabolism. It also contains no lactose.

EAT MORE Grate parmesan over soups, vegetables or pasta dishes. Shave into salads as a tasty addition. As a pre-dinner nibble with friends, make these parmesan crisps.

PARMESAN CRISPS

Preheat the oven to 180°C (350°F). Take a lightly oiled baking tray and an egg ring. Grate a mound of parmesan cheese into the ring, and then repeat until you fill up the tray.

Place the tray in the oven and bake for about 8–10 minutes. Remove and wait to cool before serving with drinks. They make a tasty alternative to potato chips.

OLIVE OIL

Olive oil is one of the star ingredients of healthy Mediterranean cooking. It is the starting base for many recipes and mostly the oil of choice for salads. Consumed in moderation, olive oil can help your body maintain a lower weight. The heart-healthy, monounsaturated fat it contains increases satiety, taming your appetite. It is necessary to eat good fat to lose fat, so don't be put off by its fat content. A simple high-fibre salad with quality protein, tossed with an olive oil dressing can be a complete meal.

EAT MORE Add olive oil and crushed garlic to blanched green beans or asparagus. Use olive oil in salad dressings, soups and casseroles and for general cooking.

BERRIES

When berries—strawberries, raspberries, blueberries and red- and blackcurrants—are in season, you will find them offered as desserts in most restaurants around France. The French hold these magical fruits in high regard, not only as a sweet treat but also as a weight management food. If you have ever had the pleasure of picking berries from a garden, you already know how wonderful they can be. Berries all contain powerful antioxidants. Mixed berries are available all year round from the freezer section of your supermarket and can be enjoyed for breakfast or as a dessert. They are high in vitamins, minerals and fibre, providing numerous health benefits. They are superb fresh when in their true season, eaten on their own or with a dollop of cream and lightly dusted with icing sugar. You can also make berry tarts or berry clafoutis for dessert.

EAT MORE Add berries to your cereal or natural yoghurt or combine frozen berries with banana and milk to make a smoothie.

9. You Don't Have to Sweat to Be Fit

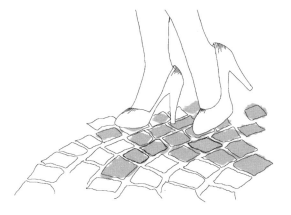

A smiling face is half the meal.

—Latvian proverb

Instead of the popular belief 'no pain, no gain', the French, not surprisingly, endorse the opposite. As hedonists, they believe there is much more to be gained, with regards to activity, when you don't put yourself through pain. Feeling good about moving means you are more likely to continue being naturally active and avoid injury. Moving is the opposite of feeling stuck—and you may feel stuck in old patterns.

Pushing their bodies to the brink of physical exhaustion is not something the French do to justify eating a pain au chocolat in the morning. Instead they walk a lot. Walking needs no prerequisites in terms of fitness levels and it's the easiest exercise to do anytime, anywhere. Few things are as effective at helping you find balance and feed your spirit as a simple fifteen-minute walk in the fresh air. Brisk walking raises your heart rate, improves circulation and can greatly boost your mood, thanks to the release of feel-good hormones that put you in a calmer, more positive frame of mind. Whether you walk in the morning, at noon or at night, notice how much more peaceful and energised you feel.

The French pursue fun activities in order to gain a better sense of wellbeing, to manage stress, to increase energy and to sleep better. They see exercise as an enjoyable pastime and a way of taking care of themselves.

I know. You're very busy—and the harder you work the less active you seem to get. Between your job, the commute to and from the job, family responsibilities, house duties, socialising and community involvements, many of you go non-stop from the minute you are blasted awake by the alarm. But how much do you actually walk? Our levels of stress have us getting too much exercise reaching into the cupboard for another cookie or the fridge for another beer.

In order to lose weight and keep it off, you only need to find ways to walk more than you currently do and be more active. There are plenty of ways to walk more, even for the busiest people. You can walk anytime, anywhere and you should. Creatively fill in the spaces of your day with walking at every opportunity. Just make sure to wear comfortable shoes. Energy creates energy, so the more active you are on a daily basis, the more inclined you will be to seek activity at every opportunity rather than avoid it.

Physical fitness is what makes you feel and look good—and have enough energy and the physical reserve to enjoy life. Be careful not to use exercise as an excuse to overeat. Even a brisk thirty-minute walk won't offset an extra large bag of potato chips.

The French have mastered slotting activity seamlessly into their routines and making it fun, which allows them to stay slim without rigorous exercise. The focus is more on how it feels to move your body, rather than on the calorie-burning effect. You should have the ability to do your work all day and the reserve to go home and play some tennis, go for a swim, walk the dog or play with the kids—and enjoy it. The idea that you must spend your free time working out at the gym several times a week, and then feel guilty when you don't, is a foreign concept to the thin French people. (But if you really do enjoy the health club, you are more likely to want to continue, especially if you feel motivated by watching others exercise too.) Anyone who is physically fit should feel able to do whatever he or she wants and not get sluggish or tired. You should be active enough to have the reserve to meet an emergency, such as running across the road to avoid getting hit by a bus, but you don't have to train like an elite athlete to be slim.

The goal in being active is to move at every opportunity throughout your day. Try walking to the shops instead of driving, get a bike and ride it when you can, get off the train or bus a few stops earlier and walk to the office. Every little bit adds up. Did you know that if you watch a sixty-minute television program at night, you will encounter twenty minutes of repetitive advertisements? Why not try cleaning the house while the ads are on! That's twenty more minutes of movement you wouldn't ordinarily get, plus the added bonus of a clean house.

The French understand that if you push your body to its limits while exercising and then get injured, you might end up not being able to move at all. The philosophy of balance, moderation and variety applies to exercise as well as eating. But that is not to imply that they are lazy, nor do they lie around watching television for hours on end. Walking is one of the best exercises as it is low impact, great for your legs, convenient and doesn't cost a thing. It is an essential part of the French way of life and in big cities such as Paris is far easier and less stressful than driving a car.

While living in Paris, walking was my main form of transport, along with the metro—even catching the subway requires a lot of walking up and down stairs and dodging the crowds through what seem like endlessly long tunnels.

Overall, I averaged one to two hours of brisk walking a day, but it was not all at once—it was spread out over the entire day. Although Josianne did her walking in heels, she would have averaged an hour a day of brisk walking too. Wearing comfortable shoes is imperative if you want to walk more, so take a change of shoes with you to make walking more enjoyable. Climbing stairs is another wonder for your figure—now, whenever I can, I take the stairs instead of the lift.

The fact is you already 'exercise' all day every day just by moving from A to B. The key to supercharging your metabolism and speeding up the rate at which your body burns energy through fat and calories is simply to move more than you are currently doing.

The home offers more opportunities for exercise than any health club. With the sweeping, mopping, scrubbing, polishing, pruning, washing and weeding, it offers exercise for every muscle in the body. You may just need to augment the effort you put into everyday chores in order for it to be a beneficial workout. For example, when vacuuming give some extra work to your thighs by doing half squats. In short, as you work around the home, use your imagination to employ as much of your body. If you do love going to the gym, by all means stick with it. But if you are paying for a membership you don't use, resign and find something you do love to do.

Exercise is a wonderful way to unwind, to let off steam, to invigorate oneself, to get together with friends or to get out of the house. It should not be considered a form of self-punishment or torture—you should exercise only for your own pleasure. Whether it be running, walking, swimming, tennis, bike riding, yoga, pilates, Latin dancing or going to the gym, only do what makes you feel good because you will be more likely to do more of it and reap the benefits of moving your body.

10. Eating Out, Parties and Holidays

At a dinner party one should eat wisely but not too well, and talk well but not too wisely.

—W Somerset Maughan

The French are famous for their restaurants. Eating out in France is a real treat. The reason the French can eat out at restaurants and not have it harm their waistlines is because the portions are small and they never rush through the meal.

The food served in a typical bistro is usually good quality and seasonal, as the customers expect, so they don't have to overeat in a search for satisfaction. A small serve of an excellent dish will, and should, satisfy all the five senses.

Even after eating a three-course meal in a French restaurant, I never felt stuffed or bloated—eating the appropriate portion size is the key when eating out. In France, servings are kept small, but portion sizes vary dramatically across different countries, so you may want to order less with the view to ordering more, according to where you are dining. As an example, a portion of rich chocolate terrine served as dessert in a Paris restaurant would typically be no bigger than a box of matches and a wedge of cheese would be about the size of two dice.

In some countries, a serve of rich chocolate terrine could easily be the size of three boxes of matches, so you could effectively find yourself eating more than you need to feel satisfied, just because it's put in front of you. The French serving sizes may seem miniscule to many people, but because there are several courses, diners don't want to get too full—then it is difficult to really enjoy the food yet to come. When you choose heavier foods, you should feel satisfied with a much smaller quantity.

When you dine out at restaurants, you may need to rethink your perception of 'value for money'. Most of what you are paying for is the 'total experience' of being pampered, served, cooked and catered for and having someone to clean all your dishes up after you've eaten. If you consider the décor, the setting, the ambience, the music, the flowers and the candles, you can better appreciate the total experience, which is what you are paying for. If you feel enriched by and appreciate the finer details of eating out, you will be less inclined to feel the need to eat beyond comfort, just to get your money's worth.

I remember dining out with a group of French women in Paris at a refined, sophisticated restaurant in the eighth arrondissement, an area often referred to as the 'Beverly Hills' of Paris. Given that the price tag was going to make a dent in my hip pocket, I felt compelled and determined to finish every last morsel of exquisite food. I was delighted when my slim French friends obviously enjoyed the food as much as I did. There was certainly no pushing food around the plate or hesitation about the bread basket. Instead everyone enjoyed three courses and a glass of wine or sparkling water.

But what I found interesting was when the waiter presented a delicate plate of petit fours after the dessert course with coffee. Without even a second thought, I dived on the plate, only to suddenly catch all eyes on me. It turns out most of my dinner friends were pleasantly satisfied after dessert (as I was) and just didn't feel the need or the inclination to push themselves beyond comfort by stuffing in more chocolates. They knew there would be other days, future meals and plenty of opportunities to eat petit fours again. My friends figured that just because it's put in front of you, doesn't mean you have to eat it. I silently asked myself, was this 'noble resistance of temptation' or simply a difference in cultural food psychology?

It made me rethink my own instinctive habits. Eventually this relaxed attitude turned out to be contagious, and I slowly learned to remain attuned and responsive to my inner signals of satiety.

In other countries, the general philosophy when eating out seems to be 'the bigger the better'. Depending on where you live and eat out, often restaurants aim to offer more value to the customer in order to win clientele over the competition. Consequently the portions sizes are simply too large, especially if you feel compelled to clean your plate and you have been conditioned since childhood not to be wasteful when it comes to food. If you struggle with this habit, you may need to check your fullness level in the middle of your meal, and be prepared to leave some food if you are no longer hungry—only you can be the judge of how much food you need. Sharing plates of food is a good option. If you struggle with waste, order less with the aim of ordering more if need be. Doggy bags are not often used in Australia, but in America and other countries they are a great way to avoid the pressure you may feel to finish everything put in front of you.

Beware of the all-you-can-eat buffets, or any deal that encourages eating until your tummy hurts. Not surprisingly, such deals are unheard of in France, except when they are offered as a tourist trap. If you do find yourself eating at a buffet for a set price, make sure to peruse the entire spread before you select your food. You do not want to see how many times you can load up and gobble down. Only eat what you really love or aim to assemble a sample plate for yourself. Be sure to save room for dessert and coffee, especially if there is a sweet you've got your eye on.

Wherever you live, dining at restaurants and socialising with friends is a fundamental part of a fulfilling life and should not have to be avoided even when trying to lose weight. It seems a shame to decline an invitation to dinner just because you fear that all the food on offer will be too 'fattening'.

Such occasions just require more planning and thought in the crucial stage when you are losing weight and learning to change old habits. If you stay listening to your body, eating as a response to hunger and respecting fullness, you are not failing. Perfection is not possible—or necessary. You will not suddenly gain weight from one meal or even one day of eating. It's what you do consistently over time that matters. You don't have to eat 'perfectly' all the time.

In Australia, as with so many cultures around the world, we use eating as an excuse to spend time with the people we like. Rather than meeting up just to talk, we catch up over breakfast, lunch, dinner or coffee. But just because you are at a restaurant, a café or at someone's house, doesn't mean you have to eat. You can simply order a drink (preferably sugarless), talk a lot and listen a lot. No-one will even notice that you are not eating because they are too busy feeding themselves. If you are hungry, by all means order something you love—and savour it. If you are not hungry, don't feel obliged to eat just to be polite.

The French are famous for lingering for hours at sidewalk cafés, talking, socialising, people-watching and just contemplating life, but often they don't actually eat anything. Typically, they may order an espresso, which often comes with a tall glass of water, but the social part is in the talking, listening and the people-watching—not always in the eating. You don't have to eat in order to socialise with friends and enjoy yourself. Although if you do go to a party, get carried away and overindulge with the excitement of the occasion, don't beat yourself up. Notice how you feel the next day after overeating, and let that be your lesson. An occasional night of splurging within reason will not make you fat, and you can always compensate the next day by eating lightly. It's all about balance.

There are a few important points to remember when you are eating out and socialising:

YOU ARE IN THE DRIVER'S SEAT, so decide in advance what is worth splurging on and what you can do without. It is helpful to have a game plan when faced with lots of tempting items. The waiter is not there to tell you what or how much to eat and drink, so make sure you're the decision-maker. Nor can the host or hostess impose any more food on you if you have had enough. Politely, graciously, take your entitlement back. Let your internal signals of hunger and satiety guide you.

ALWAYS BE PREPARED FOR THE WORST-CASE SCENARIO—as in you may not actually get to eat until a couple of hours after leaving home and arriving at the restaurant or party. That means you may be tempted to drink too much alcohol on an empty stomach, nibble too many fatty nuts and crisps or try to make a meal out of the bread basket. To avoid arriving ravenous or having to wait hours for dinner, prepare yourself by eating either a cup of vegetable soup, a hardboiled egg, a tub of yoghurt or a few pieces of cheese before you leave home. A little serving of real food should sustain you until the main meal arrives. It saves ruining your appetite on 'air food' like chips, dips and deep-fried nothings.

WATCH THE PORTION SIZES IN RESTAURANTS It seems the less you pay the more food you get, and the more you pay the less you actually get. Therefore, use your intuition and don't feel the need to scrape your plate clean if you have had enough. Consider whether eating a whole lot of cheap food really is a bargain. You can always share your main meal with someone or order a starter and salad or a side serve of vegetables. Try sharing a dessert too.

Frederic and I regularly dined out with Josianne and her husband Alain. Often it would be a three-course affair, stretched out over a leisurely two or three hours, but we never left the restaurant feeling stuffed. Order three courses if you want, but don't also eat the entire bread basket, drink a bottle of wine, add two sugars to your coffee and finish every last mouthful of dessert. Be selective, be guided by your internal cues and stick to just one glass of wine.

TRY TO DRINK VERY LITTLE during your meals, as you may drown your gastric juices and upset the digestion process. Just sip your wine rather than gulp it — wine is not intended to quench your thirst, it is meant to enhance the pleasure of the meal. If you are thirsty, drink water.

My French mother Josianne coached me on a few tricks to use when we were out at functions together. If you love parties, like I do, but want to make it through the festivities without gaining five kilograms in a month, there are a few tricks to learn. These tactics are for when you join in the fun but still want to wake up feeling great the next day and fit into your favourite jeans comfortably.

AT A COCKTAIL PARTY OR WEDDING If you want to keep your alcohol consumption to a minimum, accept the glass of champagne you have been given on arrival and hold it in your hand for a while. Touch it to your lips occasionally — you don't actually have to drink it — and then eventually set it down somewhere. Ideally, place your drink in front of one of those heavy drinkers who will always confuse their drink with yours, especially when it is full, and walk away. When the aromatic deep-fried nibbles start being passed under your nose, keep both hands busy, drink in one hand and clutch purse in the other hand. After all, if dinner is to follow, you don't need to fill up too early or eat twice! It is best to avoid drinking too much on an empty stomach anyway, as the alcohol will go straight to your head. Better still, opt for a sparkling water to begin and save the alcohol to enjoy with the meal.

AT A FRIEND'S HOUSE FOR DINNER, it is best to be gracious and accept what is served, especially if your host has gone to a lot of effort to prepare a lovely meal. However, you are by no means expected to eat it all—even etiquette experts would agree. If the food is delicious, savour every morsel mindfully, but restrain yourself from taking a second or even third helping. Wait as long as possible before you drink any alcohol because even being slightly intoxicated may result in a loss of judgement and encourage you to disrespect your body. And getting drunk will inevitably cause you to lose touch with satiety and eat more than your body needs. You still want to be able to zip up your jeans easily the next day. The best exercise you can do is to push yourself away from the table before you overeat.

ENJOYING AN ALL-YOU-CAN-EAT HOLIDAY

The winter months in Paris can get cold, grey and dreary. It's the time when most busy, hardworking Parisians will do anything to take a break from the chaos of the city. It's also the time when people hibernate and eat heavier, richer, more comforting foods, get less exercise and gain some weight. But whatever the season, if you keep paying attention to your hunger and fullness cues, you can protect yourself from acquiring unnecessary extra padding over the colder months. Wherever you live, there are probably tempting treats available on every street corner. In Paris, the scent of warm, buttery pastries teases your nostrils at every corner.

So how do you refrain? By making a plan to eat a balanced breakfast, with a view to eating a good lunch, these temptations lose their power because you don't feel hungry or deprived. With this mindset, I managed to enjoy an all-you-can-eat holiday without gaining a kilo.

After settling in to our own apartment, Frederic and I decided to take a holiday to sunny Agadir, a seaside resort town on the south coast of Morocco. Since it was such a good deal, we booked a complete package, with all meals and drinks included. Effectively it meant we could eat ourselves silly if we wanted to and return to Paris with a surplus five kilos as a souvenir.

In the past the all-you-can-eat buffet scenario would have spelled disaster for my waistline (I remember how I enthusiastically attacked buffets and ate with abandon in America). Yet I was able to truly enjoy the scrumptious Moroccan cuisine, pastries and pancakes included, even when surrounded by an abundance of choices and lavish displays of food. I thoroughly enjoyed the sumptuous buffets, but without taking any extra baggage home with me.

When people go on holiday and the food is included, with no additional charges, many feel the compulsion to eat as much as they possibly can at every meal. In the dining room of the hotel, I watched people of all nationalities hauling large plates of food back from the buffet and drinking like fish, because they had to get their money's worth. Yet we live in an abundant food environment, every day of our lives, and we have the opportunity to make our own choices about food and eating. When your mind and body stay connected and work as allies, you come to realise there is never a legitimate reason to overeat.

I made sure to peruse the entire buffet before selecting anything. After serving myself small portions of what looked great, I savoured every morsel slowly and attentively and ate what I wanted—but not more than I needed. With great food available everywhere all the time, I felt content to wait until I actually got hungry, until my senses were sharpened, so that I could truly enjoy the aromas, flavours and textures of my food. As the buffets were amazing every day, I selected what I truly loved most and skip the rest. If a dish disappointed me, I didn't bother with more than one bite. I didn't need to worry about missing out on anything because the food kept showing up every day and it looked just as good as the day before. I enjoyed sipping a glass of wine with dinner, but didn't continue guzzling to become unconscious. I woke up every morning with a clear head and a healthy hunger, ready to get the most out of each day.

I let go of the concept of eating up to get my money's worth. When I felt satisfied and nourished, I felt good, it was enough. Eating more than I needed would not only be a waste, but it would end up on my waist. When I finished each meal feeling pleasantly content, it meant I wanted to take a leisurely stroll along the beach after dinner instead of collapsing on the bed like a beached whale. When I ate until I felt comfortably satisfied, I wanted to swim, play tennis and run on the beach because it felt great to be active and outdoors in the sun. The French lessons I had learned in Paris proved not only to be transportable but were easy and made me feel good.

The mindset of eating with balance, moderation and variety while staying attuned and responsive to my inner satiety cues could be comfortably maintained, even when I was faced with elaborate buffets of free food.

I didn't need to diet before the holiday and I didn't need to diet after it either. By listening carefully to my body, I didn't need to count, weigh and measure my food. I didn't have to completely avoid entire food groups or alcohol. There was no need to beat myself up with feelings of guilt and regret because I had become an expert at trusting my own body rather than following rules.

When you learn to trust yourself and eat from an attitude of abundance rather than scarcity, you realise that just because it is put in front of you, doesn't mean you have to eat it. When you know you can have more food of your choosing again when you are hungry, there is no reason to eat like it's the last supper. The more you eat, the less flavour. The less you eat, the more flavour. Next time you go on an all-you-can-eat holiday, remember to ask yourself: if you are no longer hungry, then why are you still eating?

11. How to Nurture Yourself Without Food

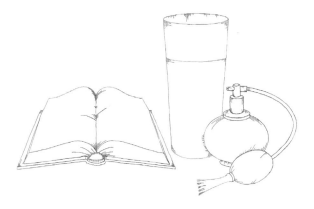

The French ... bring to their consideration of the table the same appreciation, respect, intelligence and lively interest that they have for the other arts, for painting, for literature, and for the theatre.

— Alice B Toklais

Now you have this awareness of the connection between mind and body, it's time to put food into its proper perspective. You may have used food to cope by overeating. But it's time to explore new ways to support yourself without food.

Creating a beautiful life so that every day you feel nurtured is achieved by creating meaningful personal rituals, as they help to eliminate the dullness of routine. The French are especially fond of their personal rituals which enrich and elevate the events of life and at the same time provide comfort. It may be a morning stroll through the park to buy the paper, a morning coffee at your favourite café, a laugh with a friend or a lunch date with your lover. We can all benefit from establishing rituals which help to define ourselves as humans. They are chances to create beauty, nourish our souls and to treasure the days of our lives. Special moments of self nurturing are what memories are made of. Yet how many days go by until you remember to really give yourself the attention you deserve?

When you realise that you are your own best friend, you begin to replace self-loathing with loving understanding. You know you are not perfect, but you don't care. You know how to stand by yourself in difficult times, because you love and value yourself no matter what happens. You can look inside yourself and see what's there, knowing that your feelings and perceptions are not worthless. You know who you truly are and still accept yourself with unconditional love. You respect yourself and have gratitude for your physical body, the only one you were blessed with. When you know you are worthwhile, you are able to stop your denial and recognise the times when what you really need and want is not food.

Often the desire to eat more than your body needs is really a response to an underlying need to be nurtured. Few of us have led storybook lives, but you can stop using food as a crutch, lay aside blame and guilt and get the support you need now from the people around you. With modern life so busy for many of us, it is easy to fall into the trap of 'all work and no play', so you are left with little time and a deficit of ways to amuse, pamper, stimulate, unwind and show yourself love in non-food ways.

When your first response to coping with a problem and/or rewarding yourself is to reach for food, it is usually comfort food, the type that leads to weight gain. It feels good temporarily, until the feelings of regret set in. I know.

You've had a hard day at work, the kids are screaming, the chores are building up, the creditors are calling and the toilet plumbing is clogged. It's true—we all experience disappointments and some catastrophes. You can eat to avoid feeling pain—or you can learn to face your problems, work through your feelings and grow from your experiences. You can become more compassionate, more understanding and more empowered by feeling your feelings instead of deadening them with food. This is why you would benefit from developing a repertoire of ways to nurture yourself without food.

While living in France, I started to develop more of an awareness of the many hungers we have as humans, most of which I had always tried to fulfil through food. We have heart hunger, creative hunger, hunger for knowledge, sensual hunger, hunger for beauty and spiritual hunger. Understanding the many different hungers we have that need nurturing allowed me to develop strategies to fill me up without filling me out.

My partner Frederic was the first person to confront me on my incessant need to use food as the answer to everything. It was a coping strategy I developed very early on in life and was automatic behaviour for me. Awareness of the problem was the first step in resolving the issue and better understanding my needs led me into new realms of interest and pleasure. So many diet books focus on eating certain foods at certain times, but neglect to offer strategies for feeding ourselves as a whole, even at seemingly invisible levels. We are not one-dimensional, so we shouldn't ignore the invisible, deeper emotional dimensions we all have.

As humans we are naturally curious and our hunger for knowledge needs to be nurtured continuously throughout life. Instead, many of us stop learning and developing intellectually the minute we hang up our schoolbags. Yet reigniting a thirst for knowledge and learning new things is a great way to stimulate yourself mentally and avoid the hidden trap of 'boredom eating'. So many people say 'I eat when I'm bored'. I know how it feels, because I used to do the same. But if you're not physically hungry, there are so many ways to feed your mind and cure boredom without consuming any food.

In Paris I was constantly stimulated mentally by learning a new language. The challenge of perfecting my French proved to be a great way to occupy my mind. Games like scrabble and crosswords puzzles can engage you too. Perhaps try learning a foreign language, especially if you have dreams to travel. Read an absorbing book or listen to an audio book with headphones while you go for a walk. If boredom is an issue that leads to mindless eating, whatever your passion is, explore it a little more. Whatever your age, it's never too late to develop new hobbies to occupy your interest. Crafts such as knitting and painting are not only rewarding but will keep your hands busy too.

Thanks to Frederic's influence, I developed an interest in art, architecture and historical monuments, which stimulated my hunger for visual beauty. Every Sunday, we visited places like Monet's garden at Giverny, the palace at Versailles, the Louvre and the Georges Pompidou Centre. We drove through Paris at night and marvelled at the spectacular beauty of the Eiffel Tower, the sweeping elegance of the River Seine, with its centuries-old arching bridges and admired the twinkling lights of the Champs Elysees. We walked to the top of Sacre Coeur in Montmatre, admired the breathtaking views of Paris, visited Picasso's museum and strolled through the Jardin de Tuilleries. In short, I feasted on the beauty of Paris and my surrounds, nurtured my hunger for visual beauty and mental stimulation and in the process discovered so many ways to feel vibrant and alive without a single calorie. Try exploring your city with the eyes of a tourist. And look at the countryside or the seaside — they can be breathtaking when you really stop to enjoy the moment.

I also began to develop new ways to relax and to pamper myself, which I should have done instinctively, given that

I worked in a day spa and was in the business of pampering. But I realised I had always put myself at the bottom of the list. Like the painter who never gets around to painting his own house, I realised it was important to start taking care of my own needs.

I began to prioritise my own self-nurturing and got great advice from the Frenchwomen I worked with. My French colleagues never felt guilty about treating themselves to a new lipstick, face cream, sexy lingerie or a new pair of earrings—in fact such treats are considered a necessity rather than an indulgence. They shared with me yoga poses, herbal tea flavours, classic recipes and the best brands of bubble bath. I learned where to get a great blow-wave, how to massage my own feet, where to buy the best scented candles and learned to get a kick out of listening to Edith Piaf. I began to realise that the *petit plaisirs* we offer ourselves on a daily basis play a big part in enhancing our overall sense of wellbeing.

Mastering ways of spoiling yourself without food is a great way to change your reward system. By understanding what to do when what you really need and want is not food, you open up a whole new neural pathway and begin to feel fully nourished without taking in one ounce of food.

Another hunger many people have, but often neglect, is a creative one. There are so many ways to satisfy your creative hunger, even if you don't feel you have any particular artistic talent. Fashion is a fantastic way to satisfy a need to express yourself creatively, assert your individuality and make a statement to the world just by what you wear. Being a fashion lover, I relished the opportunity of going to weekly fashion parades at the famous Galeries Lafayette department store. Watching these parades was a great opportunity to learn more about colour palettes and clothing styles. I could also walk the streets for hours on end just window shopping—I really admired the creative talent of the window dressers. In France, what you wear says a lot about you and an interest in clothes and fashion is a nurturing creative outlet for many French men and women.

Being creative can extend to the home as well. The French have the instinct to create beauty, especially in their homes. They don't think about beauty and finishing touches only when others are watching—they care about them for themselves. When you love the environment you live in and make the effort necessary in having aesthetically pleasing décor, you are in fact nurturing yourself. When you forget about trying to be perfect and remain open and willing to learn, you can try your hand at painting, photography or craft projects—they are all ways to nurture yourself creatively without food. If you play a musical instrument, get reacquainted with it and write some songs. If you love words, try your hand at poetry or writing in a journal.

Probably one of the most undervalued and underappreciated sense is the sense of smell. Yet nurturing your sense of smell and taking the time to 'smell the roses' actually enhances your sense of wellbeing. So often we forget to really smell our food. I remember reading that just smelling chocolate can be almost as pleasurable as eating it. Staying attuned to a sense of smell and using it as another type of pleasure in daily life can enhance your sense of joy.

While in France, I developed a really strong 'nose'. I got to know cheeses, perfumes, wines and chocolates, just by fine tuning my sense of smell. One summer, I even signed up and completed a perfumery course in the quaint town of Grasse, near the French Riviera, where I learned how to identify base, middle and top notes, develop flavours and mix ingredients to create a product of balance and harmony. To this day, I get a lot of pleasure from a single whiff of my favourite perfume, I love the smell of freshly brewed coffee and get excited when I smell great aromas coming from the kitchen.

Like the French, I am not totally against rewarding myself with food occasionally — sometimes there is just nothing like a molten chocolate pudding. But if eating is the primary way you find pleasure and feel nurtured, then life becomes out of balance and weight gain is inevitable.

By understanding that there are so many other ways to bring yourself pleasure, without consuming unnecessary calories, you can begin to rise above the magnetic pull of the pantry and find incredible joy in ways you never thought possible.

Here is my list (by no means complete) to get you started. We all work hard and all have stress to some degree in our lives, but it is also important to pursue pleasure each day. Rather than eat away your stress, and fill the hole in your heart with food, try some of the following ideas.

Go to the movies.
Have coffee with a friend.
Soak in a warm bubble bath.
Go shopping for new clothes.
Sing at the top of your lungs.
Plan your next holiday.
Have a massage.
Meditate.
Go to the art gallery and look at half a dozen paintings very carefully.
Walk barefoot on the sand.
Go for a swim.
Listen to music.
Have a pedicure.
Lie in the sun.
Catch up with an old friend.
Read an absorbing book.
Think good thoughts, dream a little!

12. Have Your Cake and Eat It Too

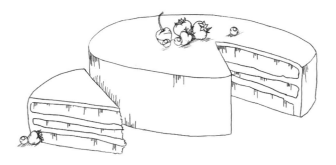

The more you eat, the less flavour—the less you eat, the more flavour.

—Chinese proverb

Believe it or not, it is possible to have your cake and eat it too, but make sure you save room for a small amount and that the choice you make is truly worth it. When it comes to chocolate and desserts, not all are created equal. Ideally, sweets should be eaten following real food, as you will need much less to feel satisfied. But be careful to allocate room in your stomach, because it is impossible to get the desired pleasure from dessert if you stuff it on top of an already uncomfortably full stomach. If you allow yourself sweet treats following real food, you will not only need much smaller amounts, but it will not affect your blood sugar levels as adversely as eating sugar on an empty stomach. By all means, allow yourself the occasional treats you really love, but not every night without scruples. I would say a couple of times a week in small portions is a reasonable plan for life.

The best way to avoid temptation is, ironically, to give in to it—which means that you never allow it too much power. As I mentioned, resistance creates force. Treat yourself little and often and then you will never have any reason to go overboard.

Cutting out all things sweet and pleasurable will only make you want to retaliate by bingeing. You can never truly enjoy your sweet treats if you keep thinking they are bad or illegal. The minute you tell yourself you can't have something; it may be all you can think about. It now controls you rather than the other way around. Therefore, the belief that all desserts have to be surrendered in order to be slim can actually end up hindering your weight-loss efforts. You don't need to give up these foods to lose weight. It just takes planning and portion control.

By cutting down portion sizes and really savouring your desserts, you will naturally find that you crave sweets less and appreciate them more. If it's special rather than commonplace, it's worth looking forward to. Now when you do decide to indulge, you will get great pleasure. You will feel satisfied with a much smaller quantity than ever before and without guilt.

Rather than look at chocolate as the enemy, as something put down on this earth to tease, tantalize and make you fat, you begin to view it in a positive way. You no longer settle for second best. You weed out all the inferior tasting brands that don't appeal to you and buy only the brand that you adore. You look forward to cherishing the experience; you let it linger on your tongue because you love the way it tastes.

By eating only the good stuff, it really hits the spot and you feel fully satisfied while consuming only little amounts. Your food talk is positive and non judgemental. Many of my French friends adore chocolate and desserts, and by giving themselves permission to eat only those delicacies that really appeal to them, mindfully and in an inviting setting, they manage to indulge selectively, on occasion, without gaining weight. If you happen to visit Paris and observe slim French people eating exquisite, decadent desserts in quaint cafes, rest assured, it will be balanced out over a whole week and compensations will be made accordingly.

It is necessary to work out the best system, one that works for you and then stick to it. When it comes to sweets, our decisions are very much driven by emotions. We think we are being rational, but we can't underestimate the importance of getting a handle on our emotions. Devise your own personalised 'food rules' that fit your needs and desires because every individual has a different need when it comes to comfort foods. For example, if you prefer to eat a small piece of dark chocolate every day, then plan ahead and perhaps eliminate bread with dinner or forgo that second glass of wine or piece of cheese. If you can go without chocolate on a daily basis, you may prefer to save the pleasure of a delicious dessert for the weekend or for special occasions, knowing that such indulgences are pure bliss when truly savoured and enjoyed as something special.

The French make mouth-watering, exquisite desserts and interestingly consume a significant amount of chocolate per capita, so the key to eating sweet treats without gaining weight is first to give yourself permission. With permission, you are more likely to choose quality over quantity and avoid unconscious, mindless consumption. When you know you're going to let yourself eat what you truly love, you definitely want to make it worth it, so you head for the best and forget the rest.

Learning to trust yourself in the presence of chocolate, cookies, cakes and ice-cream takes training. The philosophy I learned while living in France is to plan on having a sweet treat, but to just have small amounts following real food. This way, your blood sugar levels are not affected as dramatically, and because you are already satisfied by a balanced meal, you are content with the smallest amount. It took several months before I learned to keep sweet treats in the cupboards without focusing on them every time I was hungry. For you, the trigger may be chips and peanuts. Whatever it is, until you feel comfortable stocking these foods, plan on allowing yourself to have them only when out. When you arrive at a more comfortable relationship with your trigger food, their magnetic pull will no longer dominate your thoughts, so you can buy some for home and enjoy them in moderation.

Josianne stocked a cute, retro tin with rich, dark chocolate and would eat a little almost every day yet still retained her slim figure. I now eat chocolate regularly, without guilt, and I have a real ritual that goes with it.

The key to eating chocolate 'safely' is to make a little bit go a long way, for maximum pleasure and enjoyment. As a chocolate aficionado, I have participated in a few chocolate workshops and one master chocolatier, of whom I am a big fan, told me there is an art to eating chocolate in order to appreciate its true quality.

When you eat chocolate, never chew it. Instead, let it melt in your mouth slowly. A top-quality chocolate will have a delightfully smooth consistency. I prefer to consume it at room temperature, rather than straight out of the fridge. It's fun to savour the different notes of cocoa as they unravel on your tongue and stimulate your tastebuds. Remember, it is the cocoa content that really satisfies our senses, rather than the milk fat, so choose a chocolate with a high cocoa content. Savour chocolate like you would a great wine and you can enjoy it on a regular basis without getting fat.

Like a typical French woman, it is useful to know a few basic recipes for making the end of a meal light and reviving, or for creating a rich, exciting finale.

When it comes to desserts, the idea is not to deny yourself, but rather choose something that is quite rich and rewarding so that a little slither goes a long way. Think dark chocolate mousse, tangy lemon tart or cherry clafoutis. Another option is delicious ripe fresh fruit, such as berries with a little cream, a fruit based sorbet or a delicate, thin apple tart.

The subject of dessert is very dear to me, since I am, by nature, a great appreciator of sweets, and I find them particularly enjoyable at the end of a meal. However, most of my meals end with fresh fruit or plain yoghurt. I save my indulgences mainly for weekends, eating out and for special occasions.

Everyone has a few weak spots. You just have to know how to handle them.

So aim for high quality or freshly made. Ask yourself "Is eating this worth the consequence?" Believe it or not, depending on where you are eating, some cakes and desserts are not as fresh as you would hope them to be or they may disappoint you in the taste department, so use your intuition and be selective. If you order something that doesn't live up to your expectations after two mouthfuls, put down the spoon, accept the disappointment, and just leave it. If it is not exceptional or doesn't set your tastebuds on fire with delight, then it is not worth getting fat for! Remember, only indulge if you are sure your gratification is worth the sacrifice you are making.

Some of my favourite dessert recipes—ones that I make regularly—are included for you to try. Just keep the portions small and you can indulge a couple of times a week.

THIN APPLE CINNAMON TART

Frozen puff pastry is widely available pre-rolled into almost the exact size required for this tart, making this one of the easiest desserts ever. I like to cut the pastry into a rectangle shape and score the edges lightly to make a border.

2 sheets of puff pastry, trimmed into rectangles
4 golden delicious apples, peeled, cored and halved lengthways
2 tbsp unsalted butter, melted
2 tbsp sugar, mixed with ⅔ tsp ground cinnamon

Preheat the oven to 180°C (350°F). Line one baking sheet with greaseproof paper and place two puff pastry rectangles side by side. Place one halved apple cut side down on a board and slice it as thinly as possible, crosswise. Repeat with remaining apples. Slightly fan a line of very closely overlapping slices down each rectangle, lengthwise, leaving a 5mm (¼in) border.

Brush the apples very lightly with the butter and sprinkle the sugar and cinnamon mix evenly over the apples. Bake for 40 minutes, or until golden brown. Serve with pure cream or French vanilla ice-cream. SERVES 4

DARK CHOCOLATE MOUSSE

This is a rich, decadent dessert where a little goes a long way. It is also quick, easy to prepare and providing you have top quality chocolate on hand, can be whipped up impromptu as an exciting finishing touch to a meal. It is best left to set for several hours in the fridge. However, sometimes, if time is not on my side, I cover it with plastic wrap and put it in the freezer to speed things up.

200g (7oz) dark chocolate (60–70% cocoa solids)
80g (3oz) butter
4 eggs, separated
40g (1½oz) sugar

Melt the butter and chocolate in a microwave-proof bowl. Do it in short spurts of around 30 seconds, so you don't burn the chocolate. Beat the egg whites into stiff peaks and beat in the sugar. Add the egg yolks to the chocolate and whisk, mixing thoroughly. Use a spatula to incorporate the beaten egg whites into the chocolate. Divide among ramekins or leave to set in serving bowl and let people serve themselves.
SERVES 6

CHERRY CLAFOUTIS

This is a quick and satisfying dessert that can be prepared and on the table in no more than 30 minutes. It is like a baked cherry custard. You can use defrosted and well-drained mixed berries in place of the cherries as well. As cherries have a very short season, I often use a can of black pitted cherries, well drained. All the other ingredients are usually found in your fridge or cupboard.

125g (4oz) plain flour
2 eggs
75g (3oz) caster sugar
icing sugar for dusting
250ml (8oz) milk
1 x 425g (13½oz) can of black pitted cherries, well drained
a little butter

Preheat the oven to 180°C (350°F). Place the flour and eggs in a bowl and beat together until smooth. Add the caster sugar and the milk, beating until the batter has a pouring consistency. Butter a baking dish and arrange the drained cherries in it evenly, cover with the batter and then bake for 20 minutes. As soon as you take the clafoutis out of the oven, dust it with icing sugar. Serve at room temperature. SERVES 6

HONEY, ALMOND AND RASPBERRY FROZEN YOGHURT

This light and refreshing dessert takes only minutes to prepare, but it is best made a day in advance to allow for freezing time. Frozen raspberries are widely available all year round so you don't have to wait until summer. I prefer to use a full-fat Greek yoghurt for a more luxurious finish. If time is not on your side, simply take a small glass, mix the yoghurt, honey, cinnamon and berries together gently, sprinkle with almonds and enjoy.

300g (10oz) frozen raspberries
1 tbsp icing sugar
2 tbsp honey
¼ tsp cinnamon
500g (1lb) Greek yoghurt
½ cup slivered almonds

Line a loaf tin with plastic wrap, letting the sides overhang. Place the raspberries, icing sugar, honey and cinnamon in a bowl and stir to combine, and then add the yoghurt and the almonds. Spoon the mixture into the prepared loaf tin and cover the top with plastic wrap. Leave to freeze overnight. When ready to serve, lift it out of the tin and slice. SERVES 6

TANGY LEMON TART

This tart is delicious and surprisingly easy, but I would probably leave it for the weekend or when you have some time. It involves blind-baking a shortcrust pastry shell, which may sound daunting but it is really just like baking a big biscuit.

You may choose to make your favourite shortcrust pastry recipe. Alternatively, there is some excellent frozen pastry readily available.

It is worthwhile buying a 23cm (9in) loose-bottomed tart tin, because if you like this tart, you will use it over and over.

1 sheet shortcrust pastry
4 eggs
1 tbsp lemon zest
juice of 2 large lemons
¾ cup castor sugar
½ cup thickened cream

Preheat a fan-forced oven to 180°C (350°F) — 10°C (20°F) higher if using a normal oven. Take one sheet of shortcrust pastry and use it to line a greased tart tin. Cover the pastry with foil and fill with uncooked beans or pastry weights. Blind bake the pastry shell for 10 minutes, then remove the foil and weights and return to the oven for a further 5 minutes, until golden. Cool. Reduce the oven temperature to 130°C (250°F) fan-forced (or 140°C/ 275°F normal).

For the filling, whisk the remaining ingredients in a bowl, then pour into a jug with spout. Carefully pour the mixture into the cooked tart shell and bake for 25 minutes. Cool and serve. SERVES 8

13. Adapting My French Lessons to Australia

My doctor told me to stop having intimate dinners for four. Unless there are three other people.

—Orson Welles

After three wonderful years of the sweet life in Paris, I made the decision to return home to Australia. I felt somewhat torn between two cultures, as I think most expats do, but my relationship with Frederic had run its course and it was the right time to depart. The longer we lived together, the more our incompatibilities were magnified. Leaving is never an easy thing to do, especially when you leave the magic city of Paris for the other side of the world and can't just return for a weekend visit. Yet I had dreams of pursuing further studies in Australia and a loving, supportive family to come home to.

One consolation was that I was leaving as a changed woman. Remarkably, thanks largely to Josianne and Frederic, in Paris I had been transformed from a glutton to a gourmet, from decidedly round to enviably lean, from a sloppy dresser to a snappy dresser. After years spent struggling to manage my weight through dieting, ironically quitting dieting was the best thing I ever did.

I learned to eat like my French family, in a way that I could comfortably maintain for the rest of my life. I had a newfound confidence that can't really be bought—it must be learned. I looked forward to eating great food, minus the mental struggle. I knew I was a Parisienne when I started dressing up for the quick dash to the corner boulangerie to grab a baguette. After all, in Paris image is everything and self-respect is about how you present yourself. A picture tells a thousand words.

But this sentiment penetrates deeper than the superficial, it is a learned inner confidence and self-love that the French possess and was subliminally contagious for me. I felt good about my body and my ability to manage my eating and weight without dieting. But I also realised how worthwhile it is to take the time to shop, cook and prepare healthy foods. It is not selfish to take care of yourself, to plan meals ahead and to take the necessary measures to manage stress and regulate your emotions.

Longterm weight management relies on the ability to make a mind–body connection and understand how your thoughts affect your behaviour. Food choices are closely linked with emotions, so when you put food into its proper perspective and learn to listen to your body, there is never any reason to overeat. It is often said that the French have that elusive *je ne sais pas quoi* ('I don't know what'), which makes them stand out. Most French people instinctively know how to make the best of themselves, even with their imperfections. I believe the most important thing is that you feel good—about your food choices, about your body, your work and your life—which in turn gives you confidence.

My new sense of self-confidence and self-respect made me feel *bien dans ma peau* ('good in my skin'), and it dawned on me that it is a big reason the French don't 'let themselves go' and get fat. When you seek pleasure from one of our most important life sources, food, you are more likely to seek pleasure in every aspect of your life. The French are not immune to occasionally overindulging, nor do they ignore the powerful pull of sugar, fat and salt. But they refuse to let that pull override their equilibrium. The difference is that they know how to achieve balance, by listening to their bodies and ultimately remaining in the pleasure zone with food, without the feelings of guilt attached to eating.

They are less influenced by external cues urging them to eat more than they need — and more inclined to be guided by how they feel before, during and after eating. So much of the joy of eating has been taken away from so many of us due to fear, and instead eating for pleasure has, sadly, become a lost art.

Before living and working in France, I ate so many 'diet foods' and yet was slowly getting fatter. I viewed all foods with suspicion, believing that anything 'full fat' would kill me, clog my arteries or make me fat. It took a real paradigm shift to change my thoughts. I soon realised that is it not our biology that causes weight gain, but our psychology. When we eat for reasons other than true physical hunger, often we don't know when to stop, because we weren't even hungry to begin with. When we eat to tolerate the intolerable or to tranquilise ourselves, the fix of food is fleeting, a temporary crutch. As long as we choose to ignore the underlying issues causing us to overeat, permanent weight loss seems almost impossible.

As I threw myself into my new life back in Melbourne, I was looking forward to maintaining the French dietary habits I had mastered and make them work for me outside Paris. I enrolled at university to complete a specialised health science degree in clinical dermal therapies, which led me to work in the fascinating field of non-invasive cosmetic surgery. And before too long I met a wonderful Australian, who would become my husband, a man who loved to see me eat and loved eating himself. I had two danger zones to manage: the stress of studying full time and a boyfriend who could eat and drink me under the table. But I knew better than to try to eat the 'man-sized' portions enjoyed by Simon, a sporty, duel Olympian who stands at six foot two (188cm). I also consciously tried not to use food to help me study or to help me write better assignments.

I had learned very well from the French what the right portion size is for me, so I was able to stay attuned and responsive to my inner satiety signals and loyal to my positive habits. I no longer felt any need to eat beyond comfort as there was never any reason to eat today what I knew I could have tomorrow. I wanted to remain in the pleasure zone with eating. I continued to check in regularly with my feelings to monitor my emotions and I became an expert in identifying what I was really hungry for, at any given time. When I felt physically hungry, I ate, and when I finished eating, I went about my day.

Simon and I found fun and creative ways to be active together, such as body surfing, bike riding, roller blading and walking the dog. I subtly suggested that we avoid 'pigging out' and eating mindlessly on the couch as we watched television, a philosophy he gracefully accepted and didn't even miss (too much!). When I met Simon, he was living on his own and working long hours in a corporate office job. He had always tried to eat well, but when he had trained six hours a day as a professional water polo player, he could get away with eating larger amounts. But he had maintained the habit of overeating, especially at night and often takeaway, but he was also under-exercising, so the balance was out. Sensing he was feeling less than happy about the scales not being in his favour, I helped him tweak his habits and fine-tune his eating so that he has not had to worry about getting fat.

Actually, he found my habit of setting the table with all the accoutrements and having dinner tete a tete enjoyable and romantic. I have witnessed many friends who fall in love and naturally try to keep up with their man in the eating stakes, only to be devastated by their rapid weight gain. Try establishing good eating habits early on in the relationship and remember to ask yourself one simple question before you dig in: 'Am I hungry?' If you're not, try having a drink, talking and listening while you wait for hunger. You can still enjoy the company and, after all, the food always tastes better when you are hungry.

Thankfully, the new mindset that I learned while living in Paris did not get lost in translation. It survived my return to Australia. I now look forward to shopping for food, preparing new dishes and trying new ingredients. While I am conscious of eating to honour my health, my main priority is to choose foods that I truly love and that I know will satisfy and sustain me. I never feel the need to buy 'fat-free' yoghurt, cheese, ice-cream or sweets because, in learning to trust myself, I feel much more satisfied with small amounts of the real stuff.

Because I feel good about my relationship with food, I naturally discard unsatisfying eating situations and unappealing foods. I no longer swallow my sorrow, fear, my past and my future. It is certainly liberating to let go of the invisible mental struggle I lived with for years, always torn between, 'I want to eat it', 'I shouldn't eat it', 'but I will anyway' and 'now I'm out of control'. I learned to let go of the resistance and rediscovered the art of eating for pleasure.

But how exactly did I transplant my French dietary habits and lifestyle into the Australian culture?

First of all, I make time to eat. I may not have the liberty of lingering over two-hour lunches, but I do make time for three regular and consistent mealtimes each day that last at least thirty minutes each. There are no distractions such as television, computers, newspapers or talking on the phone. I make sure to serve a variety of foods that correspond with the seasons—especially fresh fruit and vegetables—which means I look forward with anticipation to the edible delights of each season and in the process, stimulate my tastebuds all year round. By establishing a structured eating routine that fits my lifestyle, I find that hunger only comes when I expect it to, so there is no need to eat preventatively out of fear that I might get hungry at an inconvenient time.

I now understand what true hunger feels like, by learning to wait for it. True hunger grumbles and mild stomach pangs are the signal that I need to eat soon. If you eat when truly hungry, the flavours of your food are magnified. Hunger is not the oral urge to chew, chomp or suck due to anger or anxiety. It is not prowling through the pantry to find something to satisfy a mouth craving. Hunger is not thirst or low energy from lack of sleep, nor is it a feeling to be feared because — as I found out — if you eat balanced meals, you can generally last between breakfast and lunch.

In-between three balanced meals a day, I drink plenty of water and herbal teas and encourage the habit by always having supplies accessible, in my handbag, in the car, in the office or clearly visible on the kitchen bench. Sometimes, if I feel the need, I enjoy a small snack such as a half cup of Greek yoghurt or a handful of pistachios.

When it comes to being active, admittedly it is more of a challenge to walk around Melbourne the way I walked around Paris, especially if I need to travel a fair distance. Like most cities in America, Melbourne is more spread out and we in Australia are largely reliant on our cars to get around. However, I make it a rule that if I need to go somewhere less than 5 kilometres (3 miles), I either walk or ride my bike. I actually find it more pleasurable to do this than to do battle with other drivers in traffic. As Simon and I are morning people and have two young children, we get up early and enjoy the thrill of breathing the fresh outdoor air before anyone else does. It gives us the opportunity to talk, walk the dog and let the kids play at the park. After the morning walk, I notice how much more peaceful and centred I feel for the rest of the day. During the day, if I see stairs, I take them. When I clean the house, I treat it as an opportunity to bend and stretch and get the heart rate up.

As you know, I am a recovering sugar addict, but I managed to adjust my taste for sweetness just by cutting back and therefore craving the sweet taste less. I cut out all additive sugars like soft drinks, sugar in coffee, cordials and lollies. When I eat desserts and chocolate, I really savour them and keep the portions small.

When I eat out at restaurants, I stick to a few rules. In Australia, like in many other countries, the portions are often too generous for one person and more suited to someone who does twelve hours of hard labour each day. So I usually opt for a starter, share a main meal and dessert, usually just taste the bread and stick to one glass of wine. I make a conscious effort to eat slowly and eat until I feel pleasantly satisfied, not uncomfortably full.

I shop for food at the local fresh-food market and stock up on the produce that is in season. Just like I did in Paris, I avoid overbuying highly addictive processed foods, things that can leave you wanting more once you begin. Occasionally I bake my own cookies to enjoy in moderation, and I am still convinced there is nothing like homemade. And I do stock good-quality chocolate because, like Josianne, I have learned to enjoy it in small amounts, without going overboard.

The one thing I miss most about France are the warm, fresh-out-of-the-oven, thin, crusty, golden baguettes that were part of my daily diet in Paris. All around France, the demand for fresh bread is so strong, that bakers churn out warm baguettes in the morning for breakfast, again for lunch and in the afternoon. The locally available baguettes just don't have the same allure, but there are still excellent

wholegrain and sourdough breads that I do enjoy. After all,
I'm not in Paris any more. But I if I close my eyes, I can
dream of eating the perfect baguette.

14. A Week of Eating, French Style

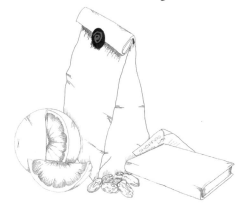

One should eat to live, and not live to eat.

— Molière

This book is not designed to tell you exactly what, when and how much to eat and exercise. I believe eating is personal and only you can be the judge of what foods really satisfy your tastebuds and make you feel your best. And how active you are is often determined by what job you have, which can in turn influence your appetite. A sedentary office job with limited physical exertion will not build the same physical hunger as a job that requires eight hours of hard labour.

Whatever your activity level, eating real, healthy foods that nourish your body and help you thrive physically and mentally should be your priority. If a healthy relationship with food is not in place first, it's difficult to pursue a truly healthy diet.

However, don't feel pressure to be a 'perfect eater' either, because life itself is not always clear-cut, so try to avoid making eating into a win or lose situation. There is no failure in learning what foods work for you and what foods work against you. The foods that satisfy me may not necessarily be what you would choose, so I can only empower you to follow your instincts and stay attuned and responsive to the wisdom of your own body.

Whether you eat meat or are vegetarian, whether you eat dairy, chocolate, cheese, bread or drink liquor is often irrelevant. However, when I coach people on how to manage their weight without dieting, they do like to get a broad picture of what a moderate, balanced eating plan looks like. I am not a dietician, and I don't believe eating is an exact science.

Being slim and healthy isn't about giving up sumptuous foods. Weight management is, at the most basic level, energy in versus energy out, so quantities of food will vary from individual to individual, according to age, sex, height and activity level.

Finding your own balance requires listening to your body, regulating your emotions, managing stress and, of course, staying consistently active. Between meals, make a habit of sticking to non-calorific drinks such as water (still or sparkling), herbal teas (warm and chilled) or tea and coffee with no more than a dash of milk. It is difficult to read true physical hunger if you fill up on liquid calories (some drinks are the equivalent of a meal), and sugary drinks adversely affect your blood sugar levels when consumed on an empty stomach.

MONDAY

BREAKFAST
coffee/tea
1 slice sourdough toast with marinated goat's cheese
1 orange
½ cup Greek yoghurt, with slivered almonds, cinnamon and
    honey

LUNCH
salad niçoise
1 small bread roll
sparkling water
2 Medjool dates
tea/coffee

AFTERNOON SNACK
handful of pistachios

DINNER
creamy veal with mushrooms
small green salad with vinaigrette
1 peach
1 small piece of dark chocolate

TUESDAY

BREAKFAST
coffee/tea
small bowl porridge with 1 tsp brown sugar
1 banana
½ cup Greek yoghurt

LUNCH
egg and lettuce multigrain roll
1 pear
1 small chocolate chip cookie
hot chocolate

DINNER
fish parcels with pesto butter
sautéed vegetables: zucchini (courgettes), mushrooms,
    red pepper (capsisum)
green salad
1 small wedge of camembert
strawberries

WEDNESDAY

BREAKFAST
coffee/tea
1 slice multigrain toast with nut spread
1 small apple
½ cup Greek yoghurt

LUNCH
slice of spinach pie
small green salad
½ cup stewed apples
2 prunes
small piece dark chocolate

DINNER
eye fillet steak with creamed horseradish
cauliflower gratin
small green salad
orange salad

THURSDAY

BREAKFAST
coffee/tea
granola, blueberry, yoghurt parfait

½ English muffin with jam
1 mandarin

LUNCH
chicken and avocado salad
1 small bread roll
½ cup yoghurt

DINNER
shepherd's pie
rocket (arugula) salad
½ fresh mango
1 small glass red wine
1 small piece dark chocolate

FRIDAY

BREAKFAST
coffee/tea
1 slice multigrain toast with herbed cream cheese
1 banana
½ cup Greek yogurt with honey and slivered almonds

LUNCH
spinach and cheese omelette
cherry tomato and olive salad
1 pear, poached or fresh

DINNER
herbed chicken tenderloins
braised cabbage with bacon
1 small glass red wine
½ cup chocolate mousse

SATURDAY

BREAKFAST
coffee/tea
2 eggs
1 small serve bacon
1 slice multigrain toast with butter
1 apple

LUNCH
eggplant (aubergine) gratin
spinach and parmesan salad
1 slice watermelon

DINNER
braised chicken with artichokes
roasted root vegetables
1 small glass red wine
1 small slice of lemon tart

SUNDAY

BREAKFAST
coffee/tea
2 eggs scrambled with smoked salmon
1 slice sourdough toast
1 pear

LUNCH
roast lamb with rosemary and garlic
spinach and parmesan salad
sparkling water
cherry clafoutis

DINNER
bowl of vegetable and lentil soup
1 small piece bread
1 small wedge camembert
½ cup Greek yoghurt

BROWN RICE PROVENCAL

This makes a great vegetarian meal. It is good to take a break from animal protein at least one night a week. I like the nuttiness of brown rice, along with the added fibre, but you can use medium white rice if you prefer.

1 cup medium-grain brown rice

2 cups chicken stock
200g (7oz) frozen baby peas, defrosted
50g (1¾oz) sun-dried tomatoes, chopped
20 olives (black or green), halved

Cook the brown rice in the chicken stock, according to packet instructions, using the absorption method. When cooked add the defrosted peas, the sun-dried tomatoes and halved olives. Mix well and serve. SERVES 2

EGGPLANT GRATIN

Eggplant can be prepared many ways. It is essential in ratatouille, delicious in moussaka and great chargrilled. I love to serve this gratin with sautéed white fish.

olive oil
2 medium eggplant, sliced 1cm (¼in) thick
250g (8oz) cup ricotta cheese
1 egg
½ cup grated parmesan cheese, plus 2 tbsp
¼ cup milk
1½ cup tomato pasta sauce
salt and pepper to taste

Preheat the oven to 200°C (400°F). Heat some olive oil in a large frypan and when hot, add several slices of eggplant and cook until browned on both sides. Place on paper towels to drain. Repeat until all the eggplant is cooked .

In a bowl, mix together the ricotta, egg, ½ cup parmesan, milk, salt and pepper. Lightly grease a medium baking dish and arrange a single layer of the eggplant, sprinkle with parmesan and ½ cup pasta sauce. Add a second layer of eggplant, sprinkle with parmesan and add the rest of the pasta sauce. Cover the top surface with the ricotta mixture, sprinkle with 2 tablespoons of parmesan and bake in the oven for thirty to forty minutes.

CHICKEN AND LENTIL CASSEROLE

This is an easy one-pot dish that, once assembled, requires no further effort while it cooks in the oven.

1 tbsp butter
½ cup diced bacon
1 onion, chopped
1 kg (2¼lb) chicken thigh fillets
1 cup brown lentils
¾ cup white wine
1 cup quartered button mushrooms
salt and pepper to taste

Preheat the oven to 200°C (400°F). Heat the butter in a heavy-based casserole dish, add the bacon and the onion and cook over high heat until browned. Add the chicken pieces and brown on both sides. Add the lentils, white wine and season well with salt and pepper. Cover with a tight fitting lid and cook in the oven for 40 minutes. Add the mushrooms and return to the oven for another 20 minutes. Serve with a side of wilted garlic spinach and crusty bread.

SERVES 4–6

BAKED RICOTTA WITH OLIVES AND SPINACH

500g (8oz) fresh ricotta
1 egg
1 clove garlic, minced
¼ cup grated parmesan
50g (1¾oz) green olives, sliced
125g (4oz) frozen chopped spinach, thawed and drained
sea salt and freshly ground black pepper

Preheat the oven to 180°C (350°F). In a bowl, mix the ricotta, egg, garlic and parmesan thoroughly and season with salt and pepper. With a wooden spoon, gently fold in the olives and the spinach. Stir well before spooning into a lightly greased 6-hole muffin tin, to about three-quarters full. Bake for about 25 minutes, until the mixture has risen, turned golden and cracked a little on top. Cool in the tin and remove carefully. Serve with salad and crusty bread.

SERVES 3–4

HOMEMADE GRANOLA

You can buy many ready-made granolas from the supermarket, but it is so easy to make your own. It will keep for a week in an airtight container and is delicious—and extremely healthy—for breakfast with some fresh fruit and plain yoghurt.

2 cups traditional rolled oats
1 cup shredded coconut
1 cup slivered almonds
1 tsp cinnamon
¼ cup vegetable oil
¼ cup honey
1 cup sultanas

Preheat the oven to 130°C (250°F). In a bowl, toss together the oats, coconut, almonds and cinnamon. In a small bowl, melt and whisk the oil and honey. Pour the liquids over the dry ingredients and stir with a wooden spoon. Spread the mixture onto a non stick baking pan and bake until golden, stirring occasionally. Depending on your oven, it could take 20–30 minutes. Cool. Add the sultanas and other chopped dried fruits, such as apricots, if desired.

CHOCOLATE CAKE

This rich chocolate cake recipe was passed on to me by my French friend Sandrine, who is a chocolate aficionado and I have been hooked ever since. It tastes even better the next day—that is, if it survives that long.

250g (8oz) dark chocolate (70% cocoa)
120g (3¾oz) butter

80g (3oz) caster sugar
4 eggs, separated (at room temperature)
½ tsp granulated coffee
2 tbsp plain flour
½ tsp vanilla extract

Preheat the oven to 180°C (350°F). Grease a loaf pan and line the bottom with baking paper. In a microwave-proof bowl, break up the chocolate and butter and melt in short spurts (30 seconds) in the microwave, stirring well until melted. Whisk in half the sugar, the egg yolks, coffee, vanilla and flour. Meanwhile, beat the egg whites until soft peaks form. Fold the whites into the chocolate mixture until no visible white streaks remain. Pour the batter into the prepared loaf tin and bake for about 30 minutes, until slightly firm in the centre. Do not over-bake. Cool in the tin.

15. Pregnancy and Feeding Children

To eat is a necessity, but to eat intelligently is an art.
—La Rochefoucauld

When I became pregnant with my first child, I admit I was
a little daunted by the impending weight gain and what it
would do to my body. When you learn the wonderful news,
the first reaction is to want to have a healthy baby. The
second thought may be a vision of yourself big, bloated and
waddling around like a mother duck.

Some women are secretly relieved that while pregnant they finally have a licence to eat whatever their heart desires without scruples and without the associated guilt. Ideally, it's best to establish instinctive, consistent eating habits and a healthy weight before conception, because it makes bouncing back after the birth less daunting and more of a natural process.

For pregnant women the accumulation of fat is not only natural, but needed, as the body builds reserves to help the foetus grow and to prepare for breastfeeding. There is no need to panic about the ensuing weight gain if you stay attuned to your body's hunger and fullness cues and honouring its needs. Your body shape will certainly change for nine months, but your eating philosophy doesn't have to.

You may want to double up on nutrition, but you don't have to double up on food. The concept of eating for two can be misleading, considering the second person is the size of a golf ball for several months. A few extra snacks throughout the day may be desired, but if you find yourself eating double or triple the quantities at every meal, then you may need to get to the underlying issue.

Once you have the baby and resume eating consciously only between hunger and satisfaction, your natural body weight will evolve in its own good time. If it took nine months for your body to change, allow at least the same amount of time for it to return to its original weight. Try not to compare yourself with the celebrities who miraculously get their pre-baby bodies back in less than six weeks!

From my experience of having two (rather large) babies and gaining around 30 kilos for each pregnancy, I know how important it is not to panic. I experienced a robust appetite all the way through each pregnancy, so I ate enough to feel satisfied. Before getting pregnant it is ideal to master not only your stress levels but eating with balance, moderation and variety. Listen carefully to the physical needs of your body with regards to food and be sure to distinguish them from your psychological needs. The inevitable hormonal roller-coaster of pregnancy can definitely play havoc with your emotions, so it is important to have a support system in place. Men can be supportive as they gear up for the rocky road ahead. If you have a mood swing every six minutes, you can always beg for forgiveness later on. Be compassionate with yourself, your energy may be depleted while your body works hard to grow the baby.

When it comes to eating, your experience will be personal. You may get morning sickness, experience strange cravings or even go off your food. Conversely, you may experience insatiable hunger like never before. For me it was definitely the latter. In order to feel good, I tried to make food choices that had some redeeming nutritional value; sharp, tasty cheese for calcium, eggs for protein, a banana for potassium, an orange for vitamin C, a handful of pistachios or almonds for good fats. As for cravings, surprisingly I went off chocolate for the entire nine months, which was highly unusual, and couldn't get enough of savoury, salty foods.

Whatever your experience, the important thing is to listen to your cravings and honour them—within reason. Your body has its own way of telling you what it needs. I needed to eat extra snacks mid morning, mid afternoon and often before bed, because I felt hungrier in general, but I also couldn't eat too much at one sitting, otherwise I felt uncomfortable with indigestion. Towards the end of the pregnancy, you may encounter puffiness, fluid retention and acute heartburn, but these are relatively fleeting in the grand scheme of things.

Breastfeeding is not only beneficial to the baby, but it is also good for the mother, as it puts the acquired fat reserves to their intended use for milk production. Breastfeeding your baby can be a wonderful ally in helping to reclaim your pre-baby silhouette. Just as important is managing the stress and emotions of new motherhood so that you can reclaim your equilibrium.

Understanding that it took nine months to gain the weight means that you need to have patience when it comes to fitting into your pre-pregnancy jeans. Allow yourself the time needed for your body to adapt. Lack of sleep may mean that you mistake the need for food for the need to rest. Checking in with your feelings to gain awareness of your emotional state is crucial in the first few months of parenthood. Lean on your partner for help or reach out to family and friends if you need support, but don't neglect to make time for your own self-care. Pack away or give away anything in your closet that no longer fits or makes you feel gorgeous now. Dowdy clothes make you feel bad and eat more. Try to enjoy the experience of new motherhood while you stay attuned and responsive to your inner satiety signals and basic needs.

The exertions of new motherhood can be a great help in burning off energy naturally, with all the lifting, bending and running around required. As long as you continue to eat between hunger and satisfaction, the excess body weight should start to melt away steadily. No two bodies are the same, so try not to compare yourself with the images of new mothers seen in the media—just keep your thoughts on your own body. A great way to relax and exercise at the same time is to take long walks while your baby sleeps in the pram. The world's easiest and cheapest exercise also helps you to calm down, lose weight and tone your thighs.

FEEDING CHILDREN

Every parent wants their child to enjoy a comfortable relationship with food, so that the kids can thrive and live the vibrant lives they deserve. With childhood obesity on the rise, I believe that modelling good eating behaviour at home is important if we want to raise healthy weighted children. Your kids may be deaf, but they are not blind. As parents you want to prevent weight problems, without causing more, so that your kids don't have to endure the teasing, name calling and shame that often come with being an overweight child.

Children are born with the innate ability to regulate their food intake and to meet their caloric needs. You can't force a baby to eat more than it needs because it will either spit it out or throw it back at you. Pay attention to when children say they are hungry or full. Regularly offer new flavours in the form of fresh foods, so that they can decide what they really love and develop a taste for fresh fruit and vegetables. Don't force children to clean their plates or bribe them with dessert for finishing their meal. As punishment for bad behaviour, don't take away their favourite foods—take away television viewing or video games. Try not to use food as a reward, instead reward desired behaviour with praise, quality time and privileges.

When your children are distressed or upset, try not to use food as a comfort—use understanding words and hugs instead. Nurture their natural talents. As they develop hobbies and creative interests that bring them pleasure and satisfaction, so they will be less likely to turn to food for fulfilment.

Communicate on an emotional level openly and freely with your children, so they become adept at identifying and understanding their own feelings, and learn to face their feelings rather than turn to food to cope. Try to put food in its proper perspective—as sustenance for living, rather than as something that will make you fat—so they learn to balance eating for nourishment with eating for pleasure. Teach your kids how to cook simple dishes and aim to get them involved in shopping, planning and preparing home-cooked meals. Show them that it is worthwhile to plan ahead so that everyone gets to enjoy delicious meals. Take them to a fresh food market and let them select some fruits and vegetables that they want to try.

Make a ritual of setting the dinner table and turning off phones, computers and television, so that you can sit down together and eat as a family without interruption. The dinner table is the perfect place to reconnect with one another, savour simple meals and share laughter, conversation and love.

Encourage your kids to develop a lifetime love of physical exercise by playing ball in the park regularly, taking family walks, playing tennis and taking bike rides together. Take them to the pool so they can learn to swim and to the park so they can learn to climb. Try to reduce the amount of time they spend in sedentary activities such as watching TV and using a computer.

Children learn by example, so try to be a positive, encouraging role model for your family. The mother is often the nutritional gatekeeper of the family, so when you as parents master the art of eating and drinking with balance, moderation and variety, you teach your kids to do the same.

16. Changing Negative Habits

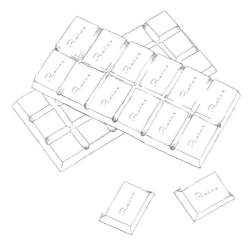

Please, sir, I want some more.

—*Oliver Twist*, Charles Dickens

So if you weren't born French, what exactly is the magical formula that promises a life of gastronomical pleasure minus the sweat and tears? I believe it begins with getting back in touch with your inner cues of hunger and satiety, and this includes learning to distinguish between physical hunger and psychological hunger. Regardless of birthplace or nationality, we were all born with this innate wisdom to eat when we are hungry and stop eating when our hunger has been relieved. Appetites can vary from day to day, according to activity levels, but given free access to food, most toddlers will consume calories according to their physical and nutritional needs.

This innate sensibility starts to degrade from about the age of three, when children are bombarded with conflicting messages from parents, peers and media about when, how much and what to consume. I've described my experience as a child—it was no surprise that by adulthood, I could no longer detect my natural biological cues.

In order to either get more love, to cope with life or to feel a sense of reward after a hard day, many people unknowingly fall into the habit of overeating. Overcoming this habit is not just a matter of discipline, because there are many well-disciplined people who continue to overeat. Most people who eat more than their bodies need do so because they have not found a way to change their negative eating habits and face the underlying issues that drive their behaviour.

To change imbedded behaviours, it is necessary to overwrite old negative ideas and install positive new programs into your subconscious—therefore changing is as much about 'unlearning' bad habits as it is about learning new ones. Believe it or not, you weren't actually born with these detrimental eating habits. You simply learned them early on. You were taught to override your body's wisdom, not to listen to your internal cues of hunger and satiety and therefore not to trust them.

We were born with the ability to eat just right, according to our physical and nutritional needs. You may believe that if you allowed yourself the liberty of eating what you truly desired, when you felt true physical hunger, you would crave only unhealthy, junky foods and would become out of control. But if you pay attention to how poor-quality food makes you feel after eating it, and to the discomfort of overconsumption, biological feedback ensures that you will inevitably gravitate towards a more balanced, healthy diet. The reason we also enjoy whole, natural foods is that they give us the energy we need to live a vibrant life. Children who are exposed to fresh, healthy, nutritional food early on naturally develop a taste for it—and it is never too late to start developing a taste for it, whatever your age. With conscious effort, you can reconnect with the innate sensibility to regulate your own appetites and weight, just by trusting the wisdom of your own body. Think of it as the 'inside out' approach to weight management.

The first step is developing an awareness and understanding of how you lost it in the first place. You need to learn how to eat consciously, inside your own awareness, while paying careful attention to your body and what it needs and wants.

With the commitment to change, the second step is becoming hyperconscious of the internal dialogue we all have running through our minds at any given moment.

Instead of criticising, try being gentle and compassionate with yourself, as every urge to overeat is an opportunity to learn more about yourself and your triggers. You need to feed your mind a diet of positive mental thoughts and eliminate the 'I'm so fat and unfit' thoughts. The most important 'food' to put into your body every morning is a positive thought. Try not to let negative internal dialogue overpower your actions and negatively affect your eating. It is necessary to learn to eat with awareness and without constantly judging yourself. When you trust yourself, you know when to stop eating.

An effective way to implement change is to try 'checking in' with your feelings before you eat, to see whether it is food that you really need. This only takes a minute or two of conscious thought. Simply close your eyes and stare at the black of your eyelids and ask yourself honestly how you are really feeling.

By checking in, you can learn ways to identify your needs when what your body and mind require and want is not food. You may be tired and need some sleep, you may have aching feet and need to give yourself a foot rub or you may feel anxious about a difficult piece of work you need to get done. More food won't help in these situations. Learning to identify your true needs on a physical as well as emotional level means you are less likely to reach for a doughnut when what you really need is a hug.

Thinking positively with an emphasis on self-nurturing is crucial to losing weight and keeping it off, because our thoughts become our beliefs, habits and automatic behaviour. We all lead busy lives, but it only takes a few minutes to practise 'checking in' and identifying your true needs. As humans, we not only have physical hunger, we have heart hunger, head hunger, spiritual hunger, sensual hunger and hunger for beauty. Not all hungers can be satisfied by food. Try getting acquainted with activities you naturally turn to when you need to be nourished without food.

Thinking kind thoughts about yourself and truly enjoying what you eat, rather than beating yourself up about it will set you on a positive path to slimness. When you understand that it is not selfish to take care of your true needs, it means that you can focus on living the full and vibrant life you deserve. Remember, you must feed your body, heart and soul, not starve them, to achieve your ideal weight. Understanding habits that were cemented in your childhood and then taking action to change them with positive replacements is the best starting point for achieving your natural, healthy weight. Change requires action, and the action is up to you.

17. Become a Thin Eater for Life

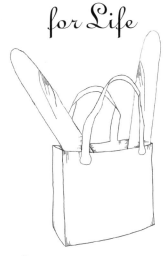

Eat little, sleep sound.

— Iranian proverb

It is one thing to do as the French do while in France, but what about translating the same mindset and positive dietary habits into your own environment? The reality is you may not have two hours for lunch, a fresh produce market down the street or be able to walk around your city easily. It may have been a while since you even turned on the oven, let alone cooked a meal from scratch. You may be aware that you eat beyond comfort regularly but feel powerless to stop.

Try asking yourself 'why' because the solution to your problem is based not only on understanding but also on action. It could simply be a negative habit, which you need to replace with a positive habit. Try to pinpoint the underlying reason causing you to make poor food choices. It may be a neglected part of you that needs nourishing. It may just be a case of 'portion distortion' as you have become out of touch or unaware of what the appropriate serving size is for you.

It is surprising how little food we actually need to survive and to feel satisfied. Many people believe that it is your biology that makes you fat—you blame your genetics, metabolism or your mother, but I believe it is more to do with volumes of food. If you constantly tried to fill the fuel gauge of your car with more fuel than it needs, it would spill out on to the pavement. Likewise, if you repeatedly feel compelled to fill your body with more food than it needs, it will spill out onto your hips. The decisions you make, with food and with life, are closely linked to your emotions. You think you're being rational, but your food choices often reflect how you really feel about your life.

When you make time for yourself, you are telling yourself that you are worth it. When you love yourself enough to look at your negative eating patterns and try to understand where they came from, you can take the necessary steps to move beyond them. When you concentrate on becoming a happier person, you understand that spending time on yourself is worthwhile. When you eat appropriate amounts of healthy food most of the time, you are reinforcing your own self-love. Take care of yourself so you can take care of others. Give to yourself freely so you know what it's like to receive.

Chances are, due to peers, parents and/or the media, you have been bombarded by conflicting messages about what, when and how much to eat so your eating patterns are chaotic and disorganised. You feel pressed for time, stressed out and overwhelmed with life. Achieving balance, moderation and variety with eating seems like an elusive dream.

The reason why many overweight people often say 'but I don't eat much' is because much of their eating takes place outside their own awareness. Often they do a particularly poor job of recalling what, when and how much they ate. I know how this feels because I used to be one of them. For years I blamed my struggle with excess weight on genetics and metabolism before I experienced the lasting results bought about by the transformation, both mentally and physically, in France.

When you learn to make the mind–body connection and get back in touch with the wisdom of your own body, your innate sensibility to detect hunger and fullness will return. If you are particularly responsive to external cues telling you when, what and how much to eat, you may feel that food controls you, rather than the other way around. But you can learn to protect yourself by simply 'tuning out'. If you start salivating the moment the hamburger or pizza commercial airs on TV, then you are allowing yourself to be vulnerable. You may even jump in the car and drive across town to satisfy a craving because the advertisement set off a signal in your brain to reward yourself. You may then eat hurriedly, guiltily, hunched over the steering wheel, while manoeuvring the traffic, all because some advertising expert hijacked your brain. But because your mind wasn't fully present with the food and you ate while distracted, you are left wanting more food. Add to that the highly addictive ingredients in fast foods and you find yourself in a vicious circle.

Start paying attention to external eating cues in your everyday environment. As a teenager, I took a job working behind the candy bar of my local cinema. It was interesting how we were told to get the popcorn machine churning out its delicious, mouthwatering aroma before patrons arrived so that they would unconsciously, like sniffer dogs, gravitate to the candy counter. The lure of buttery popcorn would be hypnotising and we would sell mountains of oversized popcorn and other junk to people who were probably not even hungry.

If external cues dictate your urge to eat when you are out, try paying attention to your personal triggers and avoiding them. I used to struggle with Mrs Fields cookies every time I walked by a stand—they were truly my Achilles heal—but I learned to put my blinkers on. Now they no longer have any power over me. They are not totally off limits, as I occasionally have one following real food—and I enjoy every last crumb—but it's a pleasure rather than a battle.

A simple shift in thinking, together with an understanding and awareness of your personal triggers, can help you to take action. When you start to address the underlying issues that cause you to make poor food choices, consume unappealing foods in uninviting settings and cause overeating, you can take steps to change. Think of it as a journey of self-discovery. You may need to rethink the amount of stress in your life, work through deep-seated issues or make more time for yourself.

The degree of success you experience in your life may well be reflected in the success you have surrounding your weight. As you take action by removing barriers and eating more healthily and as you learn how important it is to take care of yourself, the rest of your life will shift too. Taking care of yourself is modelling healthy behaviour—your actions teach our children to do the same for themselves. As Oscar Wilde said, 'To love oneself is the beginning of a lifelong romance.' You don't have to go to France to start romancing yourself, because the seed of love starts within your own heart. Besides, there are still ways of incorporating the French philosophy into your own life. You can begin the exciting changes wherever you are, because it starts from the inside, with your heart and mind.

Eating is one of the most repeated patterns in your life. When you realise that you are worth taking the time to prepare food in advance so there is something healthy to eat when you come home after a busy day, you are more likely to take time for a lunch break on even the busiest days. Not only that, you are more likely to take care of yourself in other ways too—like finding time to exercise, relax and nurture yourself without food.

My life in Australia is very different from the one I led in Paris, but I still prioritise shopping and preparing three meals a day. I try to walk whenever I can, always sit down at the table to eat and pay attention to how my stomach expands and feels fuller as I eat. I have learned to listen to my body, to trust it and to eat only when I am physically hungry rather than eating to change the way I feel.

At several points in my life, I have slowly but surely learned an effective approach to losing weight and keeping it off. It is one thing to know what to do, yet this knowledge has no power until it is utilised fully and put into action.

The action is up to you. Only you can take the first step. If dieting hasn't worked for you, there is a better solution. It literally took me years of dieting and trying some ridiculous weight loss methods to discover that the guidelines of healthy weight management are really quite a pleasure to swallow. In fact, the French paradox that intrigued me so much is not so paradoxical at all. Behind it lies a perfectly logical truth. Ultimately, when you pursue pleasure with food, and let go of resistance, you are able to eat less and enjoy it a whole lot more. Your eating patterns permeate your life and colour other activities.

Even though the French are not immune to the rising phenomenon of obesity, they have been somewhat protected by their well-established culinary traditions. These eating habits get passed on from generation to generation. Their resistance to the mass intoxication of deplorable eating habits and choosing to stick with what works for them are what I have found to be the most enjoyable and durable answer to longterm weight management. Having grown up in Australia, a country that very much follows the patterns of America, and having lived in America on a few occasions, I am convinced we can all learn something from the French approach to eating with balance, moderation and variety.

My heartfelt wish is that I have helped you to overcome the major barriers that have kept you from attaining and maintaining your ideal weight.

My experiences of learning from the French how they eat and how they view themselves and life itself has helped me to return my body and emotions to a state of balance. I lost weight—but, more importantly, I achieved a harmonious balance with food and consequently with other parts of my life. When you make time to eat, you are more likely to make food choices that work for you rather than against you. When you identify and address the underlying reasons that cause you to overeat, you'll be amazed at the relief you feel. When you plan ahead so that you have the foods you need to sustain a vibrant life and an active body, you learn to plan ahead in other areas.

Taking better care of yourself physically, mentally, spiritually and emotionally can positively affect your health, relationships, career and your ability to be happy.

Making changes to your diet and lifestyle should be embraced rather than feared, because there is no failure in learning. The most important thing is that you feel good, so go forward at your own pace.

Just as you took steps to form a negative eating pattern, you must take steps to change it. Old patterns are easy to continue. They are familiar even when they're uncomfortable. It takes time to get used to an unfamiliar action, but eventually it, too, becomes familiar. Most of us instinctively know what healthy choices are, so learning to be in tune with your body and mind, and trusting yourself to make the right choices, is what you need to aim for. Let go of ideas that have not succeeded for you in the past as you take the necessary action towards achieving your ideal weight for life. Changing your entire mindset will actually change the rest of your life. If you have learned to manage your eating, you will indeed have learned to manage your life.

Don't give up, ever.

Change can be exciting, but it can also be challenging. As Rose Tremain says, 'Life is not a dress rehearsal'. How true.

To recap the most significant points and highlight the golden rules that will enable you to master your own equilibrium, here is a summary of guidelines that you can always refer to.

- If you can't bear to waste food, it will end up on your waist, so try serving yourself a little less.

- Stop feeling stuffed, sick, bloated or guilty after eating and you will feel better than you have in a long time.
- Try sharing dishes and eating with a tapas approach, savouring small quantities of the foods you love and leaving the foods you don't.
- Not listening to or trusting your body are simply learned behaviours—unlearning them requires reprogramming your thinking.
- Every meal deserves your full attention. It is a celebration to be savoured and enjoyed.
- Believe in yourself as a slim person. Imagine the way you will look, move and dress. If you continue to think of yourself as overweight, you'll find it difficult to lose weight and keep it off.
- Diets can do more harm than good because they don't address the underlying issues that cause you to overeat in the first place.
- Learn to recognise the difference between true physical hunger and psychological hunger. Physical hunger is always satisfied by a balanced, nutritious meal. Emotional or stress-induced hunger is never satisfied by food.
- There are no 'forbidden' foods, only inappropriate quantities of certain foods. An entire cheese course in France can be the size of two dice, not a whole wheel of brie.
- When you begin to replace self-criticism with self-nurturing, you realise there is no failure in learning.

- If you are not hungry, then ask yourself why you are eating.
- Avoid eating while multi-tasking because you'll miss out on the full enjoyment of the food.
- Make less food seem like more by using smaller bowls, plates and cutlery. Aim to present your food in an aesthetically pleasing way
- Take small bites slowly, chew your food thoroughly and pause between mouthfuls. You cannot fully enjoy the bite in your mouth if another is waiting on your fork.
- Explore physical activities you enjoy—feel the way moving your body enhances your wellbeing and help to elevate your mood.
- Buy food that is in season. The food will taste better and be better value.
- A great way to eat well and pay less is to consume less. Try not to overbuy produce, have it go bad in the refrigerator and then be forced to throw it away.
- Nurture your artistic side and get creative in the kitchen.
- Keep hydrated and refreshed by drinking water and herbal teas all through the day.
- Avoid sugary drinks in-between meals because they play havoc with your blood sugar levels.
- Savour small quantities of wine with meals, but not without scruples. Treat wine like a delicacy, not gulp it down in an attempt to tranquilise yourself.

- Keep a 'mental priority list' of the indulgences you deem worth having and worth compensating for. If the (space)birthday cake at the office party appeals to you, savour it and enjoy every mouthful without guilt.
- Follow the 90–10 per cent rule. It is what you do 90 per cent of the time that makes all the difference. For the other 10 per cent, you are entitled to let your hair down.
- When you feel comfortable, set aside a 'quality treat cupboard' and stock it with the best.
- Learn what a 'just right' portion size is for you (a steak should be no bigger than the palm of your hand, not draping over the edge of the plate).
- Establish a regular eating routine that works in well with your schedule.
- Always stay in the comfort zone with food. Your body feels pain if you get overly hungry or too full.

Ultimately, the most important step towards successful results is action. The action is up to you. Every journey begins with a single step, so start slowly. Give yourself the freedom to develop a routine of your own that makes eating the right things a habit rather than a battle. Realise that you are worthy. Realise that it is worthwhile to make time for yourself to eat well, to exercise, to practise relaxation — and to spoil yourself. Give yourself the liberty to eat what really pleases you and to savour it without guilt. Love is transforming, and when it is accompanied by understanding, compassion and knowledge, that transformation can be dramatic. The love you give yourself will provide you with the strength to make permanent changes in your life.

My experience in Paris taught me so much about myself and my relationship with food. I learned that weight management doesn't have to be a battle, because when you learn to put food into its proper perspective, you learn to eat for nourishment and enjoyment. You learn to savour what you love and leave the rest. I learned this and so can you.

There is a lot of delicious food to be savoured, so be patient, be selective and always listen to the wisdom of your body. You really can have your cake and eat it too.

Index of Recipes

First published in 2011 by New Holland Publishers (Australia) Pty Ltd
Reprinted in 2012

Sydney • Auckland • London • Cape Town

www.newholland.com.au

1/66 Gibbes Street Chatswood NSW 2067 Australia • 218 Lake Road Northcote
Auckland New Zealand • 86 Edgware Road London W2 2EA United Kingdom •
Wembley Square First Floor Solan Road Gardens Cape Town 8001 South Africa

A record of this book is available at the National Library of Australia

ISBN 9781742570693

Publisher: Diane Jardine
Publishing manager: Lliane Clarke
Senior editor: Mary Trewby
Design: Lisa McKenzie
Production manager: Olga Dementiev
Printer: Toppan Leefung Printing Limited